Attack on London

Attack on London

Disaster, Rebellion, Riot, Terror and War

Jonathan Oates

Wharncliffe Books

First published in Great Britain in 2009 by
Wharncliffe Local History
an imprint of
Pen & Sword Books Ltd
47 Church Street
Barnsley
South Yorkshire
S70 2AS

ISBN 978-1-84563-056-0

A CIP catalogue record for this book is
available from the British Library.

Typeset in 11/13 Ehrhardt by Concept, Huddersfield, West Yorkshire
Printed by the MPG Books Group in the UK

Pen & Sword Books Ltd incorporates the imprints of Pen & Sword Aviation,
Pen & Sword Maritime, Pen & Sword Military, Wharncliffe Local History,
Pen & Sword Select, Pen & Sword Military Classics, Leo Cooper,
Remember When, Seaforth Publishing and Frontline Publishing.

For a complete list of Pen & Sword titles please contact
PEN & SWORD BOOKS LIMITED
47 Church Street, Barnsley, South Yorkshire, S70 2AS, England
E-mail: enquiries@pen-and-sword.co.uk
Website: www.pen-and-sword.co.uk

Contents

List of Illustrations

Acknowledgements

I wish to thank all those who have shared their reminiscences of past times with me, and all those who have assisted with my enquiries at several of London's archives and libraries, principally the Imperial War Museum, the British Library, the British Library Newspaper Library, Westminster City Archives, Wandsworth Libraries and the London Metropolitan Archives. I also wish to thank my wife, who has accompanied me on many of the research visits. Three of the pictures used in this book were reproduced by kind permission of the Museum of London, two by Reg Eden, and one by Paul Lang. Howard Ford allowed me to quote from the diary of Erica Ford. I would also like to thank Dr Robert Woolven, William Bignell, David Marr, Dr David Kynaston, John Coulter, Professor Stephen Taylor and Mrs Sarah Taylor (no relation). This book is dedicated to Sarah.

Further acknowledgements for the use of copyright material go to the following: Mrs Lavina Anson (Diary of Miss Tower); Mr Tony Benn (Diaries); Ealing Local History Centre (Diary of Henry St John); Mr Alan Thomas Goodall (Diary of Mr A.H. Goodall); Mr Allan Goodlet (Diaries of A.K. Goodlet); Mrs Dora Kneebone (Diaries of Rose Uttin); London Metropolitan Archives (Diaries of Anthony Heap); Random House Group Ltd. (*Lady Cynthia Asquith's Diaries, 1915–1918* by Lady Cynthia Asquith, published by Hutchinson); J. Stevens, *Not for the Faint Hearted*, Wiedenfeld & Nicholson, an imprint of The Orion Publishing Group; Professor John Tulloch (*One Day in July*); Wandsworth Libraries (Diaries of Florence Turtle); Evelyn Waugh, c/o Penguin Books Ltd. (E. Waugh, *A Little Learning*); Westminster Archives (Diaries of Joan Pritchard).

Introduction

This book has its origins on the Friday morning of 8 July 2005, whilst the author was on his way to work, mulling over matters of the previous day. That had been the day when terrorist bombings in London had inflicted their highest ever toll on Londoners in a single day. It had been headline news and the universal subject of conversation. My reaction was that this was, in a way, nothing new. Londoners have had far worse to contend with in the past. Apart from the Blitz, there was the Great Plague and fire of the seventeenth century. It also struck me that this would be a fine subject for a book, if one had not been written already. But the most interesting material would not concern the attacks themselves – technical details of bombs and aircraft did not excite me at all – but rather how Londoners have reacted to such dangers. My initial thought was that my fellow Londoners could take assurance from the deeds of their forebears and their fellow citizens of former times. Perhaps a greater knowledge of London's history would be helpful?

But this book is not meant as a propaganda tract along the lines of Churchill's sentiment of 'London can take it'. Rather, it is an investigation into how Londoners have coped with traumas past. It is not about, in the main, how governments and others had acted, but about the man in the street or in the Clapham omnibus.

This book begins with a brief survey of why London is so vulnerable to attack and why it has often attracted the attention of evildoers, followed by a discussion of London's defences.

There then are five large chapters, chronologically arranged. Some of these incidents will be well known – the Great Fire, the Great Plague and the Blitz mean something to most Londoners, even if only through TV and film. The five chapters consider the impact of rebellions and civil war, plagues and fires, riots, world wars and terrorism. In relating these events I have turned to eye-witnesses who recorded their experiences in letters or diaries. I have augmented these accounts with oral history reminiscences and episodes captured in the press. I have also included extracts from the diaries and letters of famous Londoners, such as John Evelyn (1620–1706), Samuel Pepys (1633–1703), Horace Walpole (1717–1797) and the novelist Evelyn Waugh (1903–1966). But there are many sources voices too: ordinary people, whose views are just as important as the great and good.

Whilst visiting London in 1814, the Prussian soldier, Prince Blücher, observed: 'What a city to loot!' His view of nineteenth-century London is applicable at almost any other time in the city's two millennia of history. Capital cities, hosting as they do, willingly or not, the seat of government and finance, provide both opportunities and dangers for those who live within their precincts ...

Threats

Controlling London was of great importance in the civil conflicts of the Middle Ages and beyond, as both the Empress Maud in the twelfth century, and 500 years later, Charles I, found to their cost. London was to be the target of rival armies from the time of Boudicca to the eighteenth century. This is partly because control of London meant control of national revenue, and those that hold the purse strings must surely triumph eventually. Governments rarely left the capital unless in dire straits. Charles II and his government left in 1665 due to the plague and set up in Oxford, and in 1683, Parliament was held in the university city, too. But these were rare exceptions. Yet, on several occasions, London was invaded by hostile forces with damage to life and property. Often, it is not the head of state who is the prime target of these attackers, but London's citizens.

London could be a dangerous place for unpopular and unwise monarchs. Charles I was a prime example of a monarch who fell foul of Londoners. So much so that one of his supporters, the Earl of Clarendon, later wrote that London was 'the sink of all the ill humours of the kingdom' and that the 'unruly and mutinous spirit' of the Londoners brought his master down. Although Charles had his enemies in the country, the violence of Londoners did have an impact on the politics of the period. Puritans and religious radicals, who identified Charles's court with the dreaded Catholics, had supporters through-out London's diverse society. Charles had to allow one of his advisers, the Earl of Strafford, to be executed in 1641 as he feared mob violence. Huge crowds roamed the streets and the King lost control of the capital early the following year. Responses of Londoners in the Civil War are explored in Chapter One. The Republican government, following the death of Cromwell in 1658, was also unpopular in London, with clashes between apprentices and soldiers.

However, London could also be a hazardous place for its citizens as well as for monarchs and government ministers. The variety of its inhabitants, often seen as an economic strength, could also be dangerous for minorities, leading to clashes and massacres. About 500 Jews were killed in rioting in 1264 and Flemish merchants lost their lives in the Evil May Day riots of 1517. As an Italian noted in 1497: 'Londoners have such fierce tempers and wicked dispositions that they not only despise the way in which Italians live, but pursue them with uncontrolled hatred.' Chapters Two, Three and Five discuss this aspect of life in London.

Bringing people together could be dangerous in other ways, too. The succession of plagues in the sixteenth and seventeenth centuries, culminating in the Great Plague of 1665 (see Chapter Two), reduced London's population, but usually not for long. London was never a healthy place, even in non-plague years. High infant mortality and crippling illnesses were common among the poor. The City government did little against these evils and usually had to be prodded into action by the government at Westminster. In fact, health issues were a major problem during most of London's history. Outbursts of disease were common throughout the nineteenth century. In 1831, over 5,000 Londoners died of cholera, and another 14,000 died in 1848–1849 of the same disease. The last cholera outbreak occurred in 1866, and another 6,000 died in London. Outbreaks of smallpox in the 1870s killed one Londoner in 2,000 – twice the national average. In the 1890s, one in five babies in poorer districts died before their first birthday. Sewerage was primitive and the water supply pitiable. Cesspools were a common sight. Early Victorian reformers, such as Edwin Chadwick and John Simon, did much in the 1840s and 1850s to make London cleaner and healthier, though not without many obstructions being posed by vested interests and the constant need for economy. And, at the dawn of the twenty-first century, diseases once thought extinct in Britain have made an unwelcome return.

Crime and the fear of crime, was ever present. Tudor and Stuart commentators were concerned about the number of vagrants, 'masterless men', who gravitated towards the capital. Many of these were migrants or discharged soldiers who had failed to find secure employment. Vagrancy became classed as a crime. Some were dealt with harshly, being whipped, branded or put in a pillory, but these punishments did not stem their number. Gangs of such desperate men worried those in authority, as they feared they could create social unrest. Theatres were also accused of harbouring criminal elements among their audiences. Yet Pepys never referred to being attacked in the streets in the 1660s, though Evelyn was robbed near Bromley in the previous decade.

The fear of crime remained in the eighteenth century. This was partly fed by the growth of the press, which was always enthusiastic to report it. Gertrude Saville, a well-to-do London spinster of the early eighteenth century, read about thieves in her newspaper, but never recorded being attacked by them. There are few statistics that give an accurate assessment of the danger posed to the law-abiding. Gangs did exist, and the thief-takers employed to catch them were often just as crooked.

It was not just professional criminals who were feared by the moneyed and propertied Londoner, as well as the government. Crowds of people – 'the mob' – could endanger property, as well as life and limb. Religion could lead to popular outbursts in the seventeenth and eighteenth centuries, with Dissenters and Catholics being singled out for harsh treatment, especially when it was thought that the government was sympathetic towards these religious minorities. Economic woes could also lead to those held responsible being attacked, whether Irish workmen in the 1730s or government ministers in the 1760s. Later in the century, the Radical movement appeared in parts of London, especially during the French Revolutionary and Napoleonic Wars and afterwards. When allied to economic difficulties, it appeared to pose a threat. The early 1820s saw a number of Radical demonstrations and then a rise in crime.

London was peaceful and safe in the early twentieth century. Yet during the General Strike of 1926 there were violent confrontations in some working-class parts of London. Criminal gangs, such as the Sabinis, were a menace in the 1920s. Certain streets were known as being dangerous for an outsider to traverse. However, total road accidents far exceeded murders in the 1920s, with over 1,000 road deaths per annum, compared with twenty or thirty murders. In the late twentieth century, criminal gangs were again dangerous and more violent, along with terrorism, which became a serious factor from the 1970s onwards. The murder rate rose, steadily, with over 150 a year in the 2000s, though overall population numbers remained constant and affluence became more general.

That said, social inequalities in London have been a fact of life for centuries. Resentment, allied with poor relations with the police, led to violent clashes in Notting Hill (1958), Southall (1979), Brixton (1981) and Broadwater Farm (1985), to name but four. In all these incidents, race was a major factor, with many (though by no means all) of those involved being Asian or black. Unpopular government policies, such as the 'Poll Tax' in 1990 and the invasion of Iraq in 2003 resulted in mass protests in Central London, though these have usually been less violent. More deadly violence came from terrorist groups: principally the IRA in the 1970s and 1980s, then Al-Qaeda in the twenty-first century.

London's Defences

London was not unprotected, though to some, it sometimes felt like it. To take law and order first. The Medieval City of London employed 200 constables to patrol the streets at night, though their effectiveness was variable and fell as the population expanded. Some parishes outside the City instituted a system of watchmen patrolling the streets at night in the eighteenth century. Their success was also variable, but there were some improvements in certain districts. The Bow Street Runners, organised by the Fielding Brothers in the 1750s and after, also enjoyed some success, but were too few to make a real impact.

The government's answer to the perceived crime wave after 1815 was to take the revolutionary step of creating a permanent civilian force of uniformed men to deter crime and to arrest evildoers – the Metropolitan Police, founded in 1829, numbering at first 3,000 men and under the control of the Home Office, not any local authority. Initially, though, they were unpopular among all classes of society. But the police were effective, in part by tolerating minor lawbreaking in order to deal more effectively with serious misdemeanours, and the crime rate fell throughout the century, though the population rose steadily. That said, there was panic in 1888 when an unknown murderer ('Jack the Ripper') slew several women in the East End and the police came in for severe criticism.

By the 1900s, the police numbered about 20,000 and by the 1980s, 24,000. The force had changed with the times, and there had been Women Police since the First World War. However, technological development was slow at times, and the force has been dogged by low-level corruption. Their employment on the street to deter crime, help the public and solve crimes, has been crucial and they frequently appear in Chapters Three, Four and Five.

Crime was not the only menace. Defence against fire was also important. During the Middle Ages and afterwards, preventative measures were left to each ward in the City, which had to provide equipment such as hooks, chains and poles with which to pull down houses in the event of a fire. Large ladders were to be kept in the houses of the wealthy (ineffective in the face of the Great Fire of 1666). In the eighteenth century, insurance companies provided fire engines to extinguish fires in the houses of those who had insured their property with them. The first public, London-wide fire service began in 1833. Yet it was only eighty men strong and they used manual fire engines when modern steam engines could have been employed. They were superseded in 1865 by the Metropolitan Fire Brigade, which availed itself of all the aids of modernity to combat fires. In the following years, twenty-six new fire stations were built throughout London. By 1921 the London Fire Brigade switched to motor fire engines as the last of the horse-drawn ones were decommissioned. To combat the forthcoming war emergency, the Auxiliary Fire Service was formed in 1939 to supplement the wartime National Fire Service. These were subsequently disbanded, but by 1980, there were almost 7,000 London firemen.

London was a walled city in Roman times and these defences helped its defenders repel enemies in the fifth century. Yet by the end of the Middle Ages, London's suburbs had grown so much that they overflowed the old city walls and no more were ever built, save the temporary defences of the 1640s (see Chapter One).

Two military formations unique to London were the Honourable Artillery Company and the London Trained Bands, both formed in the reign of Henry VIII. These citizen soldiers were active from the sixteenth to the eighteenth centuries, as we shall note in Chapters One, Two and Three.

Other military bodies of citizen soldiers were the Middlesex Militia and the Tower Hamlets Trained Bands. These were called up in times of crisis, but were probably less effective than those mentioned in the paragraph above, because they lacked training and their weaponry was variable.

Temporary aerial defences were employed during the world wars to combat the threat from the air.

Arguably, though, the most important factor in London's defences was the commonsense of the ordinary citizen. Most people do not want to see violent upheaval and few will participate in it. The number of orderly demonstrations far outweighs those marred by violence, for instance. Panic has usually been shortlived. The Londoner is a resilient creature.

London is a city of both opportunity and danger for its inhabitants, old and new. This could be said of any city, but since London is a capital city, the point is particularly valid. For instance, given that so many private and public sector bodies have their headquarters in London, employment opportunities are greater. But from the point of view of an enemy, whether domestic or foreign, it is precisely this concentration of targets that is so tempting. We shall now turn to how Londoners have responded to attacks, both directed specifically at them, or against their rulers.

Chapter 1

Early Crises 1381–1642

Without doubt very many, in the horror and consternation of eight and forty hours, paid and underwent a full penance and mortification for the hopes and insolence of three months before.[1]

Even though London has been relatively safe from foreign attack, compared with other capital cities, hostile armies from within Britain have threatened it over the centuries. This is because their leaders wanted to challenge the government and monarchy of the day, often to overthrow it or at least to alter government policy. This posed the risk of fighting in or near London, accompanied by the fear that triumphant soldiery might then plunder the city. Not all Londoners sided with the government, if course – many shared the aims of its opponents ...

The Peasants' Revolt 1381

England was in a state of turmoil in the late fourteenth century. Plague – the Black Death – had created social upheaval and the desire for political reform. The new king, Richard II (1377–1399), was only ten years old on his accession. Their troubles were not at an end. A number of poll taxes had been levied in England in the new king's reign. These were charged per head of population, in order to help finance the ongoing war in France. However, the tax of 1381 was the last straw, especially as it was set at one shilling per person: treble the previous rate. Attempts at enforcement sparked off the revolt. Added to this was the concern about French raids on the coastal towns and hostility to political mismanagement and criticism of the Established Church. Finally, there was the wish to have serfdom abolished. In June 1381 agricultural workers from across the south-east of England marched on London, camping on Blackheath prior to their final descent. Their principal leaders were Walter Tyler and John Ball.

Many Londoners sympathised with the rebels because, as ever, the capital constituted a divided society. Only a quarter of citizens had full political rights; the majority – including craftsmen and labourers – could not vote, sit on juries or hold political office. They had no reason to love the city elite and many shared the views of the rebel leaders. In fact, many mutineers were probably Londoners and, as suggested by one chronicler, coordinated their actions with those of the rural workers.

But it wasn't just London's poor who participated in the rebellion. Paul Salisbury was a wealthy citizen who had designs on his neighbour's property. During the worst of the revolt's excesses, Salisbury and a band of armed men went to the house of William Baret, who held a deed of property ownership Salisbury claimed was his by right (though not by law). Baret and his family were thrown out of their house and forced to surrender the deed. Salisbury then went to Thames Street and assaulted Joan Fastolf, whose husband had a number of property deeds Salisbury wanted. Taking these – and some alcohol – the assailants celebrated their victory.

As one might expect, most of the privileged City elite opposed the rebels. The Lord Mayor, Sir William Walworth, had sent a deputation of aldermen to meet with the rebels on Blackheath in order to dissuade them from advancing on the city. But one of the aldermen, John Horn, was later accused of encouraging the rebels to advance, claiming that Londoners would welcome them 'as a lover his loved one.' On the following day, Horn asked a city clerk to provide him with a banner bearing the royal arms. Holding the flag aloft, Horn then led the rebels into the city. Other aldermen are said to have assisted the rebels (although their names may have been blackened by political opponents): William Tongue was accused of opening the city gates, while Walter Sibley allegedly opened London Bridge.[2]

Once inside, the rebels opened prisons, sacked the Tower, ransacked the homes of the King's ministers and murdered the Archbishop of Canterbury. Monastic property in Clerkenwell was also destroyed. Many Londoners almost certainly joined with them in destroying the prisons, such as the Fleet and Marshalsea gaols. Unpopular minorities were also in great danger. Londoners attacked Flemish merchants – granted special trading privileges denied to others – chopping off their heads and displaying them on poles. Lawyers and tax gatherers – also unpopular with most Londoners – were hunted down and slain.

The mutineers also tried wringing major concessions out of the young Richard II. Walworth stood with the King when he parleyed with the rebels at Mile End. On the first meeting, the young King agreed to meet the rebels' demands. This was a crucial moment, for many of the rebels from Essex and Hertfordshire quit the revolt, thinking they had achieved their goal, but their departure only served to embolden those in London loyal to the King and Mayor.

Richard met the rebels on a second occasion, at Smithfield, on 15 June. Here Wat Tyler made fresh demands. What happened next is uncertain but the threat of violence was in the air and Walworth struck Tyler, who was later beheaded. Richard then drew the rebels northwards to Clerkenwell, allowing Walworth's men to regain control of the city. The young King's bravery had been crucial. The leaderless rebels soon dispersed and the revolt was over. Despite the young King's promises of pardons to the peasants, his political advisers had the final word and they ordered the execution of many participants. Yet the rebellion had succeeded in ending the hated poll taxes, which were not introduced again until the seventeenth century, and then only as a short-term measure.

The Peasants' Revolt has a reputation among the political Left that it does not deserve. Its memory was evoked in the late 1980s in response to the Conservative government's controversial reintroduction of the 'poll tax' (now known as Council Tax) and favourable comparisons were made between anti-government demonstrators and Tyler's rebellious peasants. This overlooks the wanton murders perpetrated by the rebels, especially the massacre of foreign merchants.

Jack Cade's Rebellion 1450
Richard II's reign ended unhappily with his deposition and murder. Yet his Lancastrian successors had variable success. By the reign of Henry VI (1422–1471), matters at home and abroad were in a sorry state. The war in France was coming to a disastrous close and Henry's government was seen as inept and corrupt. In May 1450 the men of Kent marched on London once more, this time led by Jack Cade, who went by the alias of 'Mortimer'. As before, the rebels gathered on Blackheath. By 11 June the mutineers had massed a force several thousand strong. Henry VI told them to disperse, which they did on 18 June and the danger seemed to be over. But when a detachment of the King's troops were defeated in an ambush near Sevenoaks – having unwisely pursued the rebels – the insurrection was rekindled. Inflamed by victory, the rebels marched on Southwark, hoping for support in London.

The King wished to leave London, but the city authorities – who had business links with the royal household and therefore a strong financial stake in the matter – were alarmed. Apparently, according to one contemporary source:

> the Mayor of London with the Common Council of the City came
> to the king asking him that he would stay in the city, and they would
> live and die with him, and pay for his household costs for a half year;
> but he would not, but took his journey to Kenilworth.[3]

Despite the King's desertion on 25 June, the city authorities put London into a state of defence. Gates were guarded day and night, as were wharves and lanes leading to the Thames, and ballistae (giant crossbows) deployed. Meanwhile, restrictions were placed on the sale and removal of arms and armour from the city, and agents sent to spy on the rebels.

When Cade returned to Blackheath on 29 June, the city's Common Council, after some discussion, decided to negotiate with him. The King's flight had sapped their morale, so caution became their watchword. Alderman Robert Horne was opposed to parleying with the rebels but the council slapped him in gaol. And so Alderman Thomas Cooke, a draper, went to meet Cade. He was informed of the rebels' demands – weapons, horses and money – and Cade was granted entry to London.

Cade's men entered London on 3 July, having obtained the keys to London Bridge and their numbers were soon swelled by locals. In fact, as in 1381, many Londoners welcomed the rebels, at least initially, supporting attacks on authority figures such as Alderman Malpas, an unpopular MP, whose house was plundered. In the words of a chronicler:

> They despoiled him and bore away many goods of his, and especially much money, both of silver and gold, the value of a notable sum.[4]

Cade's demands – which many Londoners thought reasonable – included political reform and the removal of the King's 'evil' advisers. Lord Saye was one of those targeted, being promptly executed by the rebels. Murder and mayhem followed, with locals joining rebels in summary beheadings and the ransacking of property. Alderman Horne barely escaped death by bribing his attackers with 500 marks. Meanwhile, Cade's political opponents were denounced at 'trials', held during Guildhall sessions to provide a semblance of legality. Although some Londoners, including Charlton, the Mayor – participated in the dubious proceedings, many judges refused to attend, leaving those present overawed by Cade's followers.

By 5 July, however, London's mood was turning against Cade. Members of the Common Council began plotting his removal, seeking help from soldiers at the Tower. Thus, on the evening of that day, locals led by Lord Scales, an experienced soldier, marched across London Bridge, armed and ready for battle. These men were probably those who had most to lose from plunder – the Mayor, aldermen and the prominent citizens. The fighting took place on the bridge during the small hours and was the bloodiest battle ever fought in London since the Boudiccan revolt. A chronicler wrote:

> And the same night the Mayor and Sheriffs and my Lord Scales and Matthew Gowghe and the Common Council of London went to London Bridge, and they fought from nine o'clock at evening till eleven in the morning, and at last the captain set the drawbridge on fire.[5]

After hundreds were killed, the rebels dispersed, encouraged by promises of pardons. Cade was eventually located and killed, his head set on London Bridge. Several of his followers were also executed. Yet, despite this reassertion of authority, Henry and his government faced a more serious rebellion in 1455, when the Duke of York's forces defeated their army at St Albans and the country slipped into periodic civil war, culminating with the fall of the House of Lancaster and the murder of Henry VI in 1471.

Londoners had been divided in their allegiances in 1450. Some shared the rebels' grievances and joined them, at least temporarily. The authorities, once the King left, were in a quandary: they were instinctively opposed to the rebellion but unsure how to deal with the threat. Once violence erupted in the streets in a drunken orgy, they were able to rally the populace and, under military guidance, defeat the rebels in open battle.

Sir Thomas Wyatt's Rising 1554

The sixteenth century was no less a time of turmoil than previous epochs. The religious policies pursued by Henry VIII and his son Edward VI were divisive, creating numerous factions of Protestants and Catholics. When the latter died in 1553 there was a contest for the throne, with the late King's chief adviser, the Duke of Northumberland, attempting to make his new daughter-in-law, Lady Jane Grey, Queen, instead of Henry VIII's eldest daughter, Mary. Yet he had little support and to the delight of Londoners, the Catholic Mary was crowned Queen in 1553. She was seen as the rightful successor following the death of her childless brother. But she courted unpopularity the following January by announcing her intention of marrying Philip II of Spain, the predominant Catholic ruler in Europe. Public annoyance was initially limited to pelting Philip's envoys with snowballs but quickly escalated into a full-blown insurrection of Kentish men, led by Sir Thomas Wyatt.

Wyatt began with only 3,000 followers – many members of the county gentry opting to stay neutral – and his chances looked slim. The government acted swiftly, ordering the Duke of Norfolk to lead the City of London's Trained Bands against Wyatt at Rochester. These citizen soldiers were among the capital's best troops, for though they were only part-time soldiers, they at least possessed proper weapons and some rudimentary training. However, the men of the Trained Bands, perhaps by a pre-arranged signal, declared their allegiance for Wyatt, shouting 'We are all Englishmen!' One of their captains advocated an immediate march on London, declaring: 'For London, they said longed sore for their coming, which they would by no means protract without breeding great peril and weakness to themselves.' When the remnant of the force retuned to London, the sight 'was almost no less joyous to the Londoners.'[6]

Many in London were clearly not sorry to see the royal forces defeated. But not all were of this view. The City made preparations to defend London. Forces of armed volunteers were formed by the livery companies of the City of London. These were mercantile companies, each representing a different trade, such as the vintners for the wine trade and so on. The borough of Southwark was ordered to furnish a bodyguard of eighty men for the Queen. Gunpowder, weapons and munitions were retained in the City. Mary was resolute in the hour of crisis and unlike Henry VI in 1450, stood her ground and remained in the capital. Her bravery inspired Londoners to rally to her defence, whatever misgivings they may have had about her religion and intended marriage. The Mayor and aldermen took it upon themselves to raise a force of 1,000 men and it was said that, at a civic dinner on the following day, the servants came wearing arms and armour. Even lawyers were so accoutred. These measures prevented Wyatt's men from progressing to the City from Southwark.

Yet many Londoners were not so supportive of Mary, especially when, on 1 February, Wyatt's men arrived at Southwark. In fact, the reception given to the rebels was enthusiastic, as a chronicler noted:

> they were suffered peaceably to enter [...] without repulse or any stroke struck either by the inhabitants or by any other [...] they all joined themselves to the said Kentish rebels, taking their part; and the said inhabitants most willingly with their best entertained them.[7]

Responses like this, however, may have been prompted by fear or lack of resolute leadership, rather than active support for the rebellion. Yet Wyatt kept his followers in check, limiting looting to the Bishop of Winchester's palace. He gained some support here from some of the Southwark men, who deserted their posts and joined Wyatt. Others just went home.

But the rebels found their immediate advance via London Bridge blocked, so they marched westwards and crossed the Thames at Kingston, site of the next accessible bridge. Eventually, on 7 February, they advanced towards Ludgate. Many Londoners were fearful. A chronicler wrote that on that morning, there was:

> much noise and tumult was everywhere: so terrible and fearful at the first was Wyatt and his army coming to the most part of the citizens who were seldom or never worst before to have or here any such invasions to the city.[8]

There was little opposition to the rebels until Ludgate was reached. Recognising Wyatt, a tailor of Watling Street had had the gates closed. Wyatt implored the Londoners to support him against the 'miserable tyranny of strangers [that] shall oppress them', but few did. The rebellion was almost at an end and Wyatt's force was overwhelmed by Loyalist forces at Temple Bar. There was little fighting. Roughly a quarter of the rebels that we know of were from London, the rest being Kentish. A total of 750 rebels were captured. Many were executed, not only Wyatt, but also Lady Jane Grey and 400 men.[9]

Despite this victory, Mary's popularity slumped when she pursued her attempts to return England to the Roman Catholic Church. From 1555, some of her Protestant opponents (about 300) were burnt at the stake. Yet the martyrs at Smithfield and elsewhere helped create a lasting memory among the Protestant English of the horrors of Catholicism. Mary was known as 'Bloody' Mary. Anti-Catholicism among Londoners was indeed to be a feature of London life for over two centuries, as we will see. Finally, it should be mentioned that Mary married Philip in 1554 but he was never crowned King of England. Mary adored Philip, but for him the marriage was a case of realpolitik, as he wanted English help in his war against France.

The English Civil War 1642
The reigns of Mary's successors, Elizabeth I (1558–1603) and James I (1603–1625) saw less political and religious upheaval, and though there was an attempted coup by the Earl of Essex in 1601 against the elderly Queen, this had little support and soon petered out. However, James's son and successor, Charles I (1625–1649) lacked the political wisdom of his two predecessors. All the attacks on and in London mentioned so far have been by forces antipathetic to the status quo, but in the autumn of 1642 it was the King's troops that were planning to march on London, not those of the rebels.

Conflict between Charles I and his enemies in Parliament, led by John Pym, reached their peak in 1640–1642. London was, on the whole, hostile to the King, forcing him to sign the order to execute the Earl of Strafford, one of his ministers, and causing Charles to believe that his family were in physical danger. The City Common Council was dominated by Charles's opponents. After trying to arrest five members of Parliament, the King and his supporters left the capital on 10 January 1642. Part of this hostility was directed against the King's political and religious policies. Anti-Catholic fears resurfaced as Henrietta Maria, the Queen, was Catholic, and there had also been massacres of Protestants in Ireland in 1641. Other factors included Charles's levying of non-Parliamentary taxes, his defeat by the Scots in the 'Bishops' Wars' and his recruitment of Irish Catholic troops, as well as rebellion in Catholic Ireland. The English Civil War had begun.

In the summer of 1642, Charles raised an army and marched towards London. There was a battle at Edgehill on 23 October. This was inconclusive, and the royal army's march south was diverted. Yet they continued towards London and planned to attack the capital from the west in the following month. This alarmed many in London. According to the Earl of Clarendon (1609–1674), a Royalist statesman and historian, 'It is certain the consternation was very great at London.' Survivors from Edgehill arrived in London and spread terrible stories. They said that Parliament's army had been routed and its commander, the Earl of Essex, was dead. They suggested that resistance was futile and that all should flee. Unsurprisingly, the whole city was full of the news of a Parliamentary defeat. Clarendon wrote that 'without doubt very many, in the horror and consternation of eight and forty hours, paid and underwent a full penance and mortification for the hopes and insolence of three months before'. But contradictory news soon arrived and a more balanced picture emerged. This calmed the anxious supporters of Parliament for a time.[10]

By early November, the King's forces were at Oxford and advanced on Reading. Essex's army was still in the Midlands. News of the situation reached London. According to Clarendon:

> This alarum quickly came to London, and was received with the deepest horror: they now unbelieved all which they had been told them from their own army.[11]

Overtures for peace then went between Parliament and the King. These came to nothing. Prince Rupert, the King's nephew, believed that the King had many supporters in London and a march on the capital would result in a speedy victory there.

But London was not undefended. The London Trained Bands, under the command of the City, were the only semi-professional body of armed men in the country. At the beginning of 1642 they numbered about 6,000 men, divided into four regiments. Parliament vested control of these troops with the radical Common Council of the City. Philip Skippon, an experienced soldier, was put in charge. By the autumn of 1642 numbers had risen to 8,000 and each man was paid twelve pence a day. Yet there was reluctance among some to enlist. On 23 September it was noted that 'a very small number of men enrolled do make their appearance, and some of them appearing do depart from their colours before they be lodged, in contempt and great neglect of the said service'. Constables were ordered to enforce attendance. In the following month, when the suggestion was made that they should be sent to guard the suburbs, 'the major part consented unto by every company, only some few did make some excuses and desired to be exempted'. Some men, though, were keen – in

October, two companies advanced as far as Windsor before being forced back by Royalist militia.[12]

Others in London were suspected of loyalty to the King. Meanwhile, some aldermen and clergy were gaoled for their lack of zeal regarding the Parliamentary cause. One was the Reverend Griffith of St Mary Magdalen, gaoled in October 1642 for preaching sermons deemed 'seditious' by Parliament.

In order to resist enemies from without, defences were put into place. Barricades were erected in the streets in case of attack. These were supervised by parish officials, who represented local government. Sheds lining the outside of the City walls were pulled down. Trenches and ramparts were constructed 'near all the Roads and highways that come to the City, as about St James, St Giles in the fields'. Women and children helped sailors dig trenches at Mile End. Parish patrols were mounted in the streets, both by day and night, and were to seize all suspicious individuals and prevent arms and ammunition passing through. Suspected Royalists were arrested. Artillery was taken from the Tower to protect the routes to London.[13]

From the autumn of 1642 to the spring of 1643, defensive works were constructed around London. It is uncertain how enthusiastic Londoners were about these, as they cost both time and money. Even so, William Lithgow thought that 100,000 civilians worked on them – an incredible number if true, as that would account for a third of all Londoners, young and old, rich and poor, men and women. According to Lithgow:

> The daily musters and shows of all sorts of Londoners here, were wondrous commendable in marching to the fields and outworks (as Merchants, silk dealers, mercers, shopkeepers &c.) with great alacrities, carrying on their shoulders iron mattocks, and wooden shovels, with roaring drummers, flying colours and swords; most companies also including ladies, women and girls: two and two carrying baskets for to advance the labour, where several wrought until they fell sick in their pains. All the trades and whole inhabitants (the Inns of Court excepted) within the City, liberties and suburbs and adjacent dependencies, went about to all quarters for the erection of their forts and trenches; and this has continued this four months past.[14]

Even though the number was probably closer to the Venetian ambassador's estimate of 20,000, the latter reported that they worked without pay and 'do not even cease on Sunday, which is so strictly observed by the Puritans'. Lithgow claimed they worked 'with great alacrity' and even members of the City's Common Council helped.[15]

Such enthusiasm was not necessarily due to their zeal for the Parliamentary cause. Rather, it may have been their fear of the Royalist army. Towns and cities often faced being looted by a victorious enemy army. The terrible sack of Magdeburg in 1631 during the Thirty Years' War in Europe was a recent example, and Parliamentary propaganda played on these fears. Preachers also encouraged their congregations. As a contemporary source put it:

> the Ministers in the City gave notice in the churches that those that were able and had good Affections to the Cause [. . .] should repair to the new Artillery Ground the next morning by eight o'clock in the morning, and they should be listed for service.

Following the defeat of a force of Parliamentary soldiers at Brentford on 12 November 1642, a Parliamentary newspaper claimed:

> But the town of Brentford was cruelly pillaged and plundered by them for they left neither beer, wine nor victuals, in all the town, and carried away all their brass, pewter, linen and other things as they could, and cut to pieces other utensils of households. Which they were forced to leave behind [. . .] they did inhumanely kill a woman being a brewer's wife, which they did when they came to plunder her home, she behaving been brought to bed but about three weeks before.[16]

Thus it was Londoners' own self-interests that dictated their responses.

Obtaining funds for the defences of London was not always easy. Many were reluctant to give money to this end. The City was forced to give funds for building but negotiated a remission, yet their payments were often in arrears. There were petitions from tradesmen about the damage that the diversion of labour and capital for the building of the defences was causing to their businesses. After all, in October 1642, Parliament ordered that all shopkeepers cease trading that 'they may with greater diligence attend the defence of London'.[17]

In late 1642 returns of London parishes were made in order to check how well they had obeyed an order from the Lord Mayor to supply Parliament with funds. It was noted that there were:

> Lists of residents in Broad Street and Vintry Wards, with their valuations, some of whom have lent money but inconsiderably [. . .] several of these returns contain also names of such as refuse or contribute not in proportion to their ability.[18]

The Royalist army marched on. By this time, part of Essex's army was at Brentford, a few miles to the west of London, with other units at Acton, 5 miles west of the capital. As said, the armies clashed at Brentford on 12 November and the Royalists were victorious. Stories of massacre and pillage by the Royalists were spread in London, but were not believed by everyone. Even so, as Clarendon wrote:

> They who believed nothing of those calumnies were not yet willing the King should enter the city with an army, which, they knew, would not be governed in so rich quarters.

London's Trained Bands were mustered on Turnham Green. In numbers they were superior to the King's forces. According to Bulstrode Whitelocke, their morale was high: 'The City Bands marched forth very cheerfully under the command of Major General Skippon, who made short, and encouraging speeches to his soldiers.' When Essex spoke to them, 'the soldiers would throw up their caps and shout, crying "Hey for old Robin." '[19] Whitelocke also reported that those in the front line were supported by non-combatants:

> The City good-wives, and others, mindful of their husbands and friends, sent many cartloads of provisions, and wines, and good things to Turnham-green, with which the soldiers were refreshed and made merry.[20]

Yet the men were not all wholly enthusiastic for the cause. Whitelocke reported that 'the City were in much trouble, and different opinions'. Parliament was also unsure where their allegiances lay and ordered that the arms of those who refused to serve be confiscated. Some later claimed that the Londoners would have given way if they had been attacked. According to Clarendon:

> I have heard many knowing men, and some who were then in the city regiments say, that if the King had advanced and charged that massy body, it had presently given ground and that the King had so great a party in every regiment, that it would have made no resistance. Yet we cannot be sure that this would have happened.[21]

However, when the opposing armies confronted each other on Turnham Green, neither felt confident enough to attack. In the end there was no battle, except for a small exchange of cannon fire. The King's forces withdrew that evening to Kingston and later to Reading. London was never directly threatened again.

Not all Londoners supported Parliament against the King, of course. But since the former had the whip hand, local Royalists had to be discreet or face arrest. The young John Evelyn recorded that, after the confrontation on Turnham Green, he wanted to join the King's forces:

> I came in with my horse and arms just at the retreat; but was not permitted to stay longer then the 15th by reason of the army marching to Gloucester, which left both me and my brothers exposed to ruin, without any advantage to His Majesty.

Evelyn and his family had property near London, which would be confiscated by Parliament should his Royalist sympathies be discovered. In the event, Evelyn spent most of the war abroad, with the King's permission. But a brief trip to London in 1643 left him dismayed:

> I saw the furious and zealous people demolish that stately cross in Cheapside. The 4th I returned with no little regret for the confusion that threatened us.[22]

Londoners' responses were never put to the test in the Civil War after 1642, as Parliament maintained control throughout and no Royalist force ever came within striking distance. It is difficult to tell how Londoners would have reacted to a major assault. There was some enthusiasm for the construction of defences, but there were others who did not share that zeal. Overall, though, Londoners' attitudes and actions were important. The loss of London was a major factor in the defeat of the King. First, it reduced his international standing, lessening the chance of any friendly foreign intervention on his behalf. Second, it deprived him of the military muscle as represented by the Tower of London and the city's Trained Bands. Finally, London was the wealthiest city in Britain and the one which, through its great trade, produced more income than any other. Of course, the great military victories of Parliament's armies at Marston Moor in 1644 and Naseby in 1645 were also decisive. Yet without the military power and money supplied by London, these could not have been possible. The possession of London was thus of great importance in deciding victory in the Civil War.

Conclusion
In all the instances given above, London's attackers were repelled by Londoners; in the first three cases, by rallying to the government. This was despite the fact that many Londoners did not approve of their monarch's policies. However, when Charles I left the capital, Londoners supported his enemies in Parliament and the City Council. In all cases, the fear of what the attacking armies might

do was an important factor in determining the reactions of Londoners. Some Londoners, of course, sided with the attackers, especially in the case of the Peasants' Revolt and in John Cade's rebellion. Private considerations, such as the settling of scores with rivals and attacking enemies, were uppermost in their minds. But generalisations about behaviour in London cannot be made, for the city's population was not united. In some cases allegiances changed during times of crisis, as in 1381 and 1450. Yet Londoners' actions in 1554 and 1642 changed the course of national history: in the one case ensuring Mary kept her crown, in the second ensuring that Charles lost his.

Chapter 2

From Restoration to Revolution
1660–1688

There was nothing heard, or seen, but crying out and lamentation, running about like distracted creatures.[1]

Londoners' zeal for the Parliamentary cause was temporary, but it was maintained until after the King's defeat in war. However, the execution of Charles I in 1649 was unpopular. The republic or 'Commonwealth' of Oliver Cromwell was expensive and failed to produce any lasting political settlement. With the death of Cromwell in 1658 there seemed little option but to recall Charles II, eldest son of the late King, in order to avert political instability. The monarchy was restored in 1660 to great jubilation in London and elsewhere. Evelyn, who observed the bloodless restoration, thanked God for it, and was convinced it was His work.

The Venner Revolt 1661

Yet there had been great political and religious experimentation during the republic, with many unorthodox religious sects coming into being. The return of the King and his conservative counsellors heralded an attempted return to pre-Civil War religious orthodoxy and the supremacy of the Anglican Church. Legislation against Protestant Dissent was therefore a burning issue.

Most Protestant Dissenters were peaceful people, but a few were not, and they reacted strongly against the new status quo. Violent religious fanatics on London's streets are, regrettably, nothing new. On the evening of 7 January 1661, Pepys recorded that:

> This morning news was brought to me to my bedside that there hath been a great stir in the City this night by the Fanatics, who have been up and killed six or seven men, but all are fled. My Lord Mayor and the whole City have been in arms, above 40,000.[2]

These religious zealots were led by Thomas Venner, a middle-aged cooper. They were Fifth Monarchy men, Nonconformist Republican radicals who had first surfaced in the previous decade, but were in decline by 1657. Venner had been plotting against the republic in the 1650s and had spent time in gaol because of it. But by 1660 he was a free man again. His aim was to conquer the world in the name of Christ, by violent means if necessary. This would also entail a revolution in the social, political, religious and economic status quo. He and his followers expected the imminent return of Jesus Christ, their slogan being: 'King Jesus and the heads upon the gates!' No wonder, then, that Evelyn referred to their 'madness, & unwarrantable zeal'. And Gilbert Burnet (1643–1715), a clergyman, wrote: 'some of them were so mad as to believe that Christ would come down and head them'.[3]

They had assembled in their meeting house in Coleman Street in the City on the previous evening, before sallying forth into the streets. Their number was small (about sixty men), but they were well armed and struck terror in Londoners for the next three days. According to Pepys 'A thing that never was heard of, that so few men should dare and do so much mischief'. Burnet wrote 'They scoured the streets before them, and killed many, while some were afraid and all amazed at this extravagance'.[4]

The first Londoner to be threatened was one Mr Johnson, a bookseller near St Paul's Cathedral. The rebels asked him for the keys to a nearby church and when he refused they simply broke the door down. They then accosted passers-by and demanded to know where their allegiances lay. When one man said he was loyal to Charles II, they shot him dead – the 'correct' answer being 'King Jesus'. Later that day there was a skirmish between the rebels and the London Trained Bands, with the former fleeing to Highgate. Apparently the rebels had first put the King's Lifeguards to flight, killing twenty of them. Soldiers examined anyone on the streets at night 'more than in the worst of times, there being great fears of these fanatics rising again.' The rebels' meeting house was demolished.[5]

The rebels were seen near Barnet on 8 January and on the following day hunger forced them to return to London. Here they hoped to seize the Lord Mayor and free any prisoners. Under cover of darkness they eluded the large bodies of militia and soldiers sent to hunt them down. This caused fresh alarms. Pepys wrote that he:

> waked in the morning about 6 a-clock by people running up and down in Mr Davis's house, talking that the Fanatics were up in arms in the City, and so I rise and went forth, where in the street I find everybody in arms at the doors.[6]

Pepys took heed and prepared himself for the worst:

> I returned (though with no good courage at all, but that I might not seem to be afeared) and got my sword and pistol, which however, I

have no powder to charge, and went to the door, where I found Sir R. Ford, and with him I walked up and down as far as the Exchange.[7]

Rumours were flying about. The men of the Trained Bands were on the streets. There were many stories about what the rebels had done. Shops were shut and 'all things in trouble'. Pepys visited his uncle in the evening and when the latter left, Pepys stayed with his aunt for some time, 'my aunt being very fearful to be alone'.[8]

Yet the rebels did not bring London to a standstill. Pepys recorded going with his wife and a friend to see the play, *The Silent Woman*, at a theatre on 7 January. They then had supper at his cousin's house. He recorded that his 'people have been very merry'. On the following night they went to the theatre again, despite fresh rumours of rebels' sightings. Sir John Reresby was interested in seeing the rebels, so he rode out from London accompanied by a servant but did not have his wish fulfilled.[9]

It was only on 10 January that the full story emerged. There had been fierce fighting in the City on the previous day between the rebels and soldiers. Sir Richard Browne, the Lord Mayor, had been active with the citizen forces, having only had two hours' sleep before being roused, donning arms and armour to lead them. One contemporary thought that it was 'through the heroical courage and brave behaviour of our prudent, famous and ever renowned Lord Mayor, these merciless and cruel tigers were soon dispersed'. It seems that by mid-morning 'the Londoners were all Alarmed and grew so numerous that they needed no Assistance from Westminster'. It was said that the men of the Trained Bands:

> were together in a ready posture and the Trained Bands stood in a public, braver hostility, which did show a great deal of loyalty and true allegiance to their Prince, whereby they have got such a mark of honour, that will remain upon their posterities unto future generations.

Victory went to the latter. The rebels fought with fanatical bravery and few surrendered. Those captured were tried and executed, including Venner himself on 19 January.[10]

Those who sympathised with the rebels were abused by fellow Londoners. One woman who spoke in Cheapside on their behalf was assaulted by stone-throwing boys. Londoners were afraid, but they were not panic-stricken, and in the end the rebels were defeated by the courage of the Lord Mayor and the citizen-soldiers of the Trained Bands. Venner's brief rebellion had strengthened the case for religious orthodoxy and in 1662, laws were passed to make failure to attend Anglican services a criminal offence.

After the defeat of the Venner Revolt, London was more peaceful and there was a degree of political stability. Dissenters were, however, banned from preaching within 5 miles of a corporate town or city, so none could legally worship there. Richard Baxter, a well-known Dissenter, was obliged to go to Acton, 5 miles from London, in order to worship.

Yet the capital soon faced worse dangers than religious Dissent. Some saw these new threats as the results of God's anger at the immorality of the newly restored court (Charles was notoriously unfaithful to his wife and caused further offence by permitting women to act on the London stage). Such behaviour was seen by moralists as all the worse because God had seen fit to rescue the country from the republic and had restored the monarchy and Church of England. Thus to live scandalous lives was doubly sinful and could only lead to a Godly rebuke, in the form of natural disasters. These were not long in arriving. They were deadly because pestilence and fire can spread rapidly among a city densely packed with houses and people. Inexpert handling of both crises added to London's woes.

The Great Plague 1665–1666

There had been outbreaks of pestilence in the capital prior to 1665. These happened principally in 1348, 1563, 1593 and 1625, and in percentage terms it was the plague of 1563 (also known as the 'Great Plague' until 1665) that was the most deadly. But that of 1665 was worse. It was also the best recorded, for two of London's greatest diarists were on hand to do so – Pepys and his friend Evelyn. In 1665, as in previous years, the whole country was hit by the plague, but London, being the most populous city by far, was the worst affected.

Contemporaries did not understand the causes of the bubonic plague or Black Death. These were only discovered in the nineteenth century. Basically it was a disease of black rats. Rats carried fleas and the deadly ones were known as *Xenopsylla Cheopis*, which could also cause human fleas to carry the plague. These fleas did not have the plague themselves but could and did infect others, including humans. They did so by injecting bacillus, causing swellings on their victims, often resulting in death within about five days. These deadly fleas could also pass from human to human by coughs and sneezes. Victims developed spots and boils, and suffered from vomiting, headaches and sickness. Many became delirious. Many thought that any contact with an infected person spelt death for them. This was not unreasonable. Contemporaries did not know how properly to treat such diseases. For instance, some thought that smoking tobacco was a preventative. A more recent scientific theory is that the plague was not bubonic plague, but a virus.

The plague may have had its origins in the Levant or in Algiers: in either case it was taken by ships along the trading routes to Europe. There were outbreaks in Hamburg and Amsterdam in 1663–1664. Over 24,000 people died of plague in the latter city in 1664. Steps were taken in London to quarantine people and goods from Dutch ports, but the system was not watertight, especially when war broke out against the Dutch in 1665. Presumably a ship managed to get past London's defences; or perhaps infected people had reached London before these measures were implemented and the disease had lain dormant till the spring of 1665. In 1665, the atmosphere in London was sultry – Pepys recorded that 7 June was the hottest day he had ever known – thus ideal for the deadly fleas, which thrive in warm weather. The plague began in London in April in the West End, reaching the City in early June of 1665. It is uncertain exactly how many people died (many deaths went unrecorded) but one estimate gives a staggering 100,000 – a quarter of London's population. Death was unequally distributed – in some parts of London, one in three died. Mortality was highest in the East End. At the height of the plague, as many as fifty people died each day in one parish. It was not just Central London that was affected. Outlying parishes such as Acton, Uxbridge and Brentford in Middlesex were also affected, as was Deptford in Kent, from early July (some 406 dying in the latter according to Evelyn). About 100 of Acton's inhabitants succumbed to the plague – roughly one in six.

Those that could quit the capital generally did so, the crisis becoming known as 'the Poor's Plague', as the lower classes had no choice but to tough it out. Charles II's chief minister, the Earl of Clarendon, wrote: 'The greatest number of those who died consisted of women and children, and the lowest and poorest sort of the people [...] not many of wealth or quality or of much conversation being dead.' Those elderly people who could remember earlier epidemics were among the first to leave London, as noted by Clarendon:

> And many of them removed their families out of the city to country habitations; when their neighbours laughed at their providence, and thought they might have stayed without danger: but they found shortly that they had done wisely.[11]

Charles II and his court set an example of flight by moving to Syon House at the end of June and then, in July, to Hampton Court, then to Salisbury, and finally to Oxford (where the court had settled during the Civil War). Many of the wealthy followed the King's lead. Poets such as Milton and Dryden fled for the countryside. Lady Sandwich went because she was 'afeared of the sickness and resolved to be gone into the country', yet delayed her flight a few weeks longer in London to see the result of a society elopement. Clergy did likewise. The Dean of St Paul's spent most of 1665 at Tunbridge Wells. Richard Baxter, a Nonconformist minister, left his wife and children at Acton while he went to stay with a friend in Buckinghamshire. Most members of the Royal Society fled London and suspended their meetings. Pepys noticed 'coaches and wagons being all full of people going into the country'. Merchants and tradesmen also left London, as well as the nobility and gentry. About 12 per cent of the residents of Westminster absented themselves.[12] Masters often left their property in the possession of their servants. The young William Taswell's parents did so. One Johanna 'a good old faithful servant' was left to tend the house whilst the family went to Greenwich.[13]

Some were uncertain whether to leave. On 22 June, Pepys recorded that his mother 'hath a mind to stay a little longer'. Pepys sympathised with the view, reasoning that in London she was free from embroilment in family affairs. Eventually she agreed to leave, but 'she was to the last unwilling to go'. When Pepys's wife left for Woolwich a fortnight later, her oft adulterous husband was, nevertheless, sad to see her depart. He wrote that he was 'grieved in my heart to part with my wife, being much worse by much without her, though some trouble there is in having care of a family at home in this time of plague'. That night he wrote 'Late home and to bed – very lonely'. Yet he left London for Greenwich on 18 August, as his department of the Admiralty was ordered to Greenwich.[14]

Not all those who fled were fortunate. At first, villages and towns charged visitors exorbitant rates to stay. Later they prevented all entry, fear of the plague overriding their greed. Refugees had to obtain certificates from parish officials, stating that the holders were healthy. This led to forgeries, with the consequence that only printed, not handwritten, forms were deemed genuine. At Guildford, wells were padlocked to prevent plague carriers using them. Oxford's gates were guarded. This resulted in refugees wandering around the country, welcomed by no one. Dr Busby had the masters and scholars of Westminster School leave London for the village of Chiswick, in order to escape the plague. However, as William Taswell, one of the scholars, later wrote: 'it spread its baneful influence even to this place.' Those who owned boats on the Thames were luckier, as they could distance themselves from the plague, and a higher proportion survived than those who stayed on dry land.[15]

Some men removed their families while themselves remaining in London. Evelyn, who lived at Sayes Court, Deptford, recorded: 'On the 4th [August], I went to Wotton [Surrey], taking thither my son and his tutor, Mr Bohun (a Fellow of New College) for fear of the pestilence, still increasing both in London and its environs. The 7th, I returned home.' Twenty-four days later he sent his young wife (who was seven months pregnant) and the rest of the family to Wotton. Only a couple of servants were retained by Evelyn. In September, a resident of Gracious Street, who had buried all his children but one, and having shut himself up in his house, had a friend remove his last child, which was taken to Greenwich. Sir Roger Burgoyne sent his children from Clapham to Warwickshire.[16]

Flight was the most rational response, for those who were able to do so. There was no known cure for the plague. Therefore, to distance oneself and one's family was clearly the most sensible step to take. It was not just the wealthy who left London, though they were more noticeable. The Dutch ambassador noted that 'Both great and mean fly the city on account of the plague.' [17]

It seemed that those who did stay, even though they could have left, did so out of duty. Evelyn wrote that he was 'resolved to stay at my house myself and to look after my charge, trusting in the providence and goodness of God'. One of his responsibilities was the welfare of Dutch prisoners of war (England and Holland were at war at this time) and this task he carried out conscientiously. He was later thanked by the King for this, but the modest Evelyn recorded, 'in truth I did but what was my duty, & that I had performed it as I ought'. Although Pepys was frightened of infection, writing on 21 July, 'the plague growing very raging, and my apprehensions of it great', he remained at work for the Admiralty. He told Sir William Coventry, 'You, Sir, took your turn at the sword; I must not therefore grudge to take mine at the pestilence', although, as noted above, he moved to Greenwich a few weeks later. Yet he took care to set his affairs in order in case of death and drew up a new will, as 'a man cannot depend on living two days'. Henry Oldenburg wrote likewise: 'I strive to banish both fear and overconfidence, leading a regular life and avoiding the infected places as much as I can, leaving the rest to God.' Sir Roger Burgoyne wrote: 'I trust God in mercy will preserve me and this family from that violent disease.'[18]

Pepys commented often about how empty fashionable parts of London were. On 22 July he wrote:

> To Fox-Hall, where to the Spring garden; but I do not see one guest there, the town being so empty of anybody to come thither. I by coach home, not meeting with but two coaches, and but two carts from White Hall to my own house, that I could observe, and the streets mighty thin of people.[19]

This was not only because people had fled the capital, or were dead, but that many avoided travelling through the streets if they could help it, in case they came into contact with anyone suffering from the plague.

Not all those in authority fled. The Lord Mayor, Sir John Lawrence, stayed in London and he forbade his aldermen to leave. Those who had already left were ordered to return. The City Fathers remained in London and passed ordinances to stop food prices rising and to prevent unemployment. Yet some of their measures were foolish in retrospect. Lawrence ordered the destruction of dogs and cats, thinking they spread the plague, when in fact they helped prevent it by catching rats. Across London, about 40,000 dogs and 200,000 cats were slain, with a twopenny bounty on each. He also ordered fires to be lit in the streets in September, attempting to dispel the plague by fumigation. Luckily the wooden buildings did not catch fire. However, these seemingly odd policies were in accordance with the best expert advice then available. After complaints were made that plague pits were becoming foul, the court of aldermen ordered that each corpse should occupy a separate grave and that no new pits be dug.

The principal response of those in authority was to try to isolate plague victims in order to prevent the plague from spreading. Some were moved to specially-constructed 'pest-houses', which were ordered to be built in mid-June. However, there were only about five of these, housing perhaps 600 people in total, and they were soon crowded. Some people were sent there by their masters. The Taswell family sent two maidservants to a public pest-house, for instance. Most people, though, were locked in their own homes, with the rest of their family, whether plague victims or not. Houses were marked and guarded. They were then quarantined for forty days. Conditions in these houses were appalling. Sometimes inmates would escape or be rescued by friends. This is what happened when the first notice was put up on a house in St Giles-in-the-Fields, 'in a riotous manner & the people of the house permitted to go abroad into the street promiscuously, with others'. Sir Thomas Peyton put the blame on this parish: 'That one parish of St Giles, London, has done all the mischief.' Taverns, playhouses and schools were closed, again to prevent the spread of the plague by curtailing social interaction.[20]

Because so many of the wealthier inhabitants had left, there was a shortfall in revenue to the parish authorities as poor rates were no longer paid by the absentee inhabitants. At a time of acute distress, this was potentially disastrous. Appeals were made for charity. *The Newes* noted:

> Whereas divers well-disposed persons have already sent (and others may hereafter send) their charitable Relief for such persons and families as at present, or such as hereafter may be visited with the Infection of the Pestilence.

Such money was directed into the hands of the churchwardens for distribution to the poor, especially those confined to their houses because one member was ill.[21]

In September, the severe policy of locking potential sufferers indoors was modified. Lawrence declared a curfew at nine o'clock, in order that sick people could walk in the streets for air. Funeral processions took place then and were attended by many people, at least forty or fifty with each one in September.

Yet some parishes were less rigorous in locking up sufferers and non-sufferers in their homes. So great was the plague in some parishes that this policy was unworkable. Some contemporaries noted sufferers in the streets in the daytime. Pepys wrote, 'so many sick people in the streets full of sores' and 'there being now no observation of shutting up houses infected'. The Reverend Patrick was critical of these people, writing, 'they ought to be more civil. But we must not expect that from ordinary People: it is a thing proper to better Bred Souls. If the Vulgar be not intolerably rude, we are beholden to them'. Clarendon blamed the spread of the plague on the fact that the quarantine system was only partially effective, though, unlike Patrick, he blamed those in authority.[22]

There was contemporary criticism regarding the system of quarantine. It was argued that conditions in these houses became so foul, as well as unpleasant and claustrophobic, that life for those inside became more dangerous. It was also pointed out that the houses were not sealed, as food and drink were taken to them. Children were sometimes removed from plague houses – William Francis, a Hackney labourer, received several children from one such house, which could have endangered the village of Hackney. He was later tried for the offence. John Hancocke of Hackney took potentially infected goods from Shoreditch and brought them into Hackney. Violence occasionally erupted. William Michell brought goods into Stoke Newington that were suspected of being from the plague-ridden parish of St Giles. He assaulted Richard Gytters, the constable, who questioned him on the matter. There was also ill will between those in the same household – one man who was infected attacked his wife with murderous intent, albeit unsuccessfully. It was alleged that inmates were neglected and left to suffer.

It is hard to know if the quarantine system was effective. Many opposed it. And there were reports concerning households where all had died, when originally only one was infected. Yet in most households only one or two died. Some people were unattractive to fleas – famously, Pepys noted an occasion when he shared a bed in Portsmouth in 1662: the fleas bit the other man while he remained unmolested. Some people shut themselves voluntarily in their houses in order to prevent the plague being spread and were esteemed for doing so. Pepys recorded on 11 July:

> I saw poor Dr Burnett's door shut; but he hath, I hear, gained great goodwill among his neighbours; for he discovered it himself first, and caused himself to be shut up of his own accord: which was very handsome.[23]

Some parish officials were diligent in their labours, sometimes at great personal cost. John Greene, High Constable of High Holborn:

> was very vigilant and diligent in the performance of his office of Constable [...] out of his own resources he expended the said money [£55 2s 6d] on the visited poor, with the encouragement of the inhabitants and Justices of the said district.

Greene visited the houses of the plague victims in order to ascertain their needs, which he reported to the Justices. Unfortunately he died in the course of his duties and his son asked to be reimbursed.[24]

Parishes appointed men to guard the infected houses. Householders were to give notice of any suffering from the plague. If there were insufficient men acting as guards, those in receipt of parish relief were to carry out this unpleasant duty or have their payments suspended. Coffins of plague victims were not to stand in church during services and children were not to approach the corpse, coffin or grave.

The doctors could do little, but could make substantial profits. They prescribed strange remedies with such names as 'Dragon Water', 'Venice Treacle' and 'Plague Water'. But although these remedies were ineffectual, Londoners, in their desperation, turned to them. They had little choice. But if the medical men were as ignorant as their patients, they were often heroic. Dr George Thomson performed an autopsy on a plague victim in order to understand the disease – and caught it himself. He survived, though, in spite of placing a dried toad on his chest. His assistant, Alexander Burnet, aided at the autopsy but, as noted above, was less fortunate and died. Some doctors fled (including Sir Edward Alston, President of the College of Physicians) but those that stayed saw their paying patients increase. William Boghurst claimed to have fifty or sixty patients each day. Some advertised in the press. Yet most people did not have access to doctors or physicians. Pepys bought tobacco to sniff and found it 'took away the apprehension'. Yet no one knew what to do for the best, Pepys recording that 'all the news is [...] of the plague growing upon us in this town; and of remedies against it: some saying one thing and some another'. He was also given 'Plague Water' to protect himself.[25]

Vendors of remedies against the plague, not necessarily apothecaries or doctors, advertised their wares in the newspapers from May 1665. Richard Lowndes, a bookseller at the White Lion, near to St Paul's Cathedral, sold, for twelve pence, 'An approved Antidote or Pectoral against the Plague, prepared by some eminent Physician, in that great Contagion of 1625, and taken with good success'. He also sold 'The late Countess of Kent's Powder', which

> has been lately experimented upon divers infected persons with admirable success. The virtues of it against the plague and all malignant distempers are sufficiently known to all physicians of Christendom and the powder itself prepared by the only person living that has the true Receipt [recipe].

He claimed he was selling this remedy at a third of the usual price. Similarly, Simon Grape, stationer in Fleet Street, sold a 'Universal Medicine and Antidote against all Pestilential and Contagious Distempers'. One doctor said that Malaga raisins, if boiled and baked, then eaten, would act as a cure.[26]

There was even a cure for the plague detailed in *The Intelligencer*. It stated that three pints of Malmesbury wine, with sage and rue, be boiled and strained. Then long pepper, a half ounce of ginger and a quarter of nutmeg should be added and boiled. Mithridate and Venice treacle was added and when cold, a quarter pint of angelica was mixed. Three spoonfuls would apparently cure an adult, but only one spoonful was needed merely to prevent infection ...

It is impossible to know whether any of these remedies actually worked. Predictably, the adverts claimed they were effective. Eustace Burneby's powder was used by the Reverend Robert Boreman of St Giles and he and his sexton, John Gerey, attested that it worked. They visited the homes of the afflicted and, some weeks later, those given the remedy recovered. Those they visited and to whom the cure was not given, died.

Pamphlets describing the plague were sold. The Reverend Patrick had written 'A consolatory discourse, persuading to a cheerful trust in God in these times of trouble and danger'. Not all such writings were explicitly religious in tone. John Gadbury sold 'London's Deliverance Predicted in a short Discourse'. This told the story of how the plague had begun and predicted when it would end.[27]

In order to protect themselves, those treating the sick wore waxed leather coats and beak-like masks containing herbs. Lawrence was encased in a glass

cylinder when he saw visitors. Others carried white sticks 4 feet long, in order
to stop any infected person coming near.

William Taswell's father did not think it amiss to ask his son to deliver
letters for him in London, though, unsurprisingly, at first the boy was reluctant.
However:

> at last my duty got the better of my inclinations, and after he had
> provided me with the herb called angelica and some aromatics,
> besides some eatables in a bag, my kind and indulgent mother giving
> me too some Spanish wine, I made the best of my way to town.[28]

Meanwhile, the apothecaries tried to improve their hitherto junior status
compared to the College of Physicians. But some of the latter stayed in London
and advertised their altruistic motives in doing so. Dr Nicholas Davis of
Austin Friars and Edward D'Avoy, both of the College of Surgeons, claimed in
the press that they:

> have thought fit upon principles of Honour & Conscience to declare
> that they are ready and willing to attend [...] and to visit all such
> persons in and about this City and counties adjacent as shall desire
> their Assistance and directions.[29]

One doctor who fled London was Dr Goddard. On his return in January
1666, he defended the conduct of fellow physicians who had done likewise.
According to Pepys, Goddard stated that 'their particular patients were most
gone out of town in the plague-time, and they left at liberty'.[30]

Some sought solace in religion. Burnet wrote that the calamities of the plague
were 'looked upon as characters of Divine wrath, and gave but a melancholy
aspect'. It was thought by some that the plague was a sign of God's displeasure
and judgement on such a sinful nation. Stephen Bing, a minor canon of
St Paul's, wrote 'People frequent the church as before' and on 3 August, civic
dignitaries and 'a great congregation' were present at church – normality
continuing in the face of adversity. Houses in Drury Lane, whose occupants
were infected, wrote on their doors, besides a red cross, 'Lord have mercy upon
us'. From early July, the first Wednesday of each month was appointed as a day
to be kept as a solemn fast and a day of humiliation in order that God would
bring the plague to an end. On these occasions, alms for the poor were
collected.

The Reverend Patrick was another conscientious clergyman. He visited the
sick, distributed alms and officiated at burials. He also collected charitable
donations in order to pay for food for those quarantined in their homes. Dr

Robert Breton, Rector of Deptford, also remained at his post throughout the crisis period, as did Archbishop Sheldon. According to *The Intelligencer*:

> His Grace the Lord Archbishop hath all this while kept his station and constantly attended all the dates of his charge and functions [. . .] in the middle of all hazard.[31]

Some worshippers, however, shunned their parish church or attended another – from September 1665 to January 1666, Evelyn attended St Alphege's church in Greenwich, rather than attend his parish church of St Nicholas's, Deptford 'for our parish was exceedingly infected'.

However, as stated, many clergymen fled the capital and some churches were shut up. The Reverend Daniel Milles, vicar at St Olave, Hart Street, was the first to leave in his parish. Burnet wrote that this was a shame, as 'people were in a more than ordinary disposition to profit by good sermons'. Even when the clergy did not flee, they shut their churches up during the plague and advised their parishioners to pray at home rather than bring people together and increase the risk of infection – sound advice. But if some of the Anglican clergy were found wanting, others were ready to step into the breach. Burnet noted:

> some of the Nonconformists went into the empty pulpits, and preached with great freedom, reflecting on the vices of the court and the severities that they themselves had been made to suffer [Nonconformists suffered penalties such as fines or even imprisonment for practising their faith].

Anglican clergy feared that the Nonconformists would preach sedition against the Established Church and State, blaming those in authority for the onset of the plague.[32]

Pepys, as curious as ever, recorded his personal reactions to the plague. He first wrote about it on 30 April: 'Great fears of the sickness here in the City, it being said that two or three houses are already shut up. God preserve us all.' On 7 June, seeing doors marked with crosses, he recorded that this was 'a sad sight to me, being the first of the kind that my remembrance ever saw', and three days later, 'to my great trouble, hear the plague is come into the City'. Oddly enough, in August, he wrote, 'I went forth and walked towards Moorfields to see whether I could see any dead corpse going to the grave'. On this occasion Pepys did not encounter any corpses, but within a few weeks such sights would be common enough. On 15 September, he wrote: 'I met a dead corpse of the plague, in the narrow alley just bringing down a little pair of stairs. But I thank God I was not much disturbed at it ...' The following month, when Pepys saw a coffin borne by mourners, he observed, 'Lord! To see what custom is, that I am come almost to think nothing of it.' As ever, he was curious to see public spectacles.[33]

Businesses closed and few ventured out. On 7 September Evelyn walked through the streets and recorded that it was 'a dismal passage and dangerous to see so many coffins exposed in the streets, and the streets thin with people, the shops shut up, and all in a mournful silence as not knowing whose turn might be next'. When Pepys was travelling along Holborn in a hackney carriage and the driver suddenly became ill, the diarist found another conveyance. He later wrote that he had 'a sad heart for the poor man and for myself also, lest he should have been struck with the plague'. He noted once that travelling by such methods 'is become a very dangerous passage nowadays, the sickness increasing mightily'.[34]

Fear led to suspicion of one's fellow man. Pepys noted 'the disease making us more cruel to one another than we are to dogs'. Pepys even records that some sufferers, locked up in their homes, leaned out of windows and breathed on the healthy, in the belief they would infect those they envied. Meanwhile, talk of the plague was on everyone's lips, 'discourse in the street is of death, and nothing else'. And few people wore new wigs, for fear the hair had come from plague victims. According to Sir Roger Burgoyne, social pleasantries plummeted: 'all people are so fearful of the sickness that they will receive none, much less people they know not.'[35]

Unemployment was another phenomenon. This occurred because of the flight of the rich. Shopkeepers went bankrupt due to loss of business. Servants who were jobless sometimes turned to crime to make ends meet. They robbed both living and dead and looted unoccupied houses. Sarah Stapleton was lying sick with plague in her house in East Smithfield, but a woman and two male accomplices 'ransacked, pillaged and carried away' her moveable property. Likewise, Elizabeth Baldwin was accused of 'having feloniously embezzled goods of John Maynston, who died of the sickness of the pestilence'. Joan Barnet was accused of plundering property from several houses. Four women were charged with stealing goods belonging to the late Dr Parker, who had died of the plague. Goods to the value of over £100 were taken by Isabella Petty when she broke into the late Richard Scavell's house.[36]

One thing that did not happen, however, despite all the fear and terror, was mass panic. People did not look for scapegoats, such as witches or Jews, or even the current national enemy, the Dutch (in contrast to their reactions against foreigners in 1666). People remained calm. This is not to say they were resigned to their fates – some fled, some tried patent medicines. But society did not break down.

It was hoped that, as summer turned to autumn and the temperature fell, the plague's effects might diminish. This did not happen and deaths in September, as recorded by the Bills of Mortality, rose by 600 to 7,165 (the highest ever recorded for a single month). Yet numbers were falling by the end of the month: 'blessed be God!' wrote Pepys. The trend of diminishing mortality rates continued in October (in spite of 4,327 deaths being recorded from the plague in one week).

Despite Pepys remarking that mournful topics dominated conversation, life went on. At the end of July he attended a wedding and recorded, 'Thus I ended this month with the greatest joy that ever I did in all my life', adding that one reason for this was that he had saved money! On 10 September he met friends at Greenwich. Evelyn was also there and Pepys recorded that he 'did make us all die almost with laughter'. Finally, Pepys's Plague year was over: 'to my great joy.'[37]

Many shops were closed but business continued at the Royal Exchange. In September, Pepys recorded: 'I did wonder to see the 'Change so full, I believe 200 people; but not a man or merchant of any fashion, but plain men all.' By October this had helped to restore some confidence. In November, Pepys and Evelyn met there and discussed nothing more sinister than a collection of sixteenth-century letters.[38] By November, optimism was more justified as deaths from plague continued to fall. According to *The Newes*:

> This week it has pleased God to make a sure abatement of the mortality in this City. And we have now great reason to hope (Blessed be God for it) that the time of mercy is at hand, when the Lord will remove this heavy judgement from among us and in a few weeks more restore this City to its former health and happiness.

Hard frost was expected to reduce deaths even further. Pepys wrote: 'I was very glad to hear that the plague is come very low.' The cold weather, it was hoped, was playing a decisive part in reducing deaths caused by the plague.[39]

As indicated, deaths from plague began to subside in late September 1665, causing a drift back to London in December. By this time, Pepys was recording that plague deaths had dropped 'almost to nothing', and shops began to reopen. According to *The Intelligencer*, by the end of November there was an 'abundance [of people] returning out of the countries whither they had retired themselves during the heat of the contagion'. And Pepys could record with joy on 5 January 1666:

> But Lord, what staring to see a nobleman's coach come to town [...]
> And a delightful thing it is to see the town full of people again, as it is

now, and shops begin to open, though in many places [. . .] all shut;
but yet the town is full compared with what it used to be.

Next day Pepys's wife returned. Yet there were few gentry in town and the
court was still absent. Clarendon wrote, with a little exaggeration:

> nobody who had left the town had yet the courage to return thither:
> nor had they reason; for though it was a considerable abatement from
> the height it had been at, yet there died still between three and four
> thousand in the week.[40]

There was still concern. On a meeting of Pepys and his colleagues on
8 January, the diarist noted, 'we met first since the plague, which God preserve
us in'. The second week of January saw a slight increase in plague victims.
Pepys noted: 'if the plague continues among us another year, the Lord knows
what will become of us.' Yet, despite such fears, life returned to normal as
plague deaths fell dramatically. But times were changing for the better. Pepys
made many visits to old haunts and saw old friends for the first time since the
plague began.[41]

In February 1666 the King, his brother, his uncle and his council, moved to
Hampton Court in order to more effectively govern the country, though the
rest of the court remained at Oxford. Even though the King was not back in
London, the very fact that he was closer to the capital was a fillip to Londoners'
morale. As one contemporary put it: 'there was a strange universal joy there
was for the king's being so near.'[42]

By the end of the month, the King finally returned to London. This
heralded a return of the wealthy to the capital. Clarendon wrote:

> it can hardly be imagined what numbers flocked thither from all parts
> upon the fame of the King being at Whitehall, all men being ashamed
> of their fear of the plague when the King ventured his person.[43]

Evelyn's family also returned, the diarist noting:

> Blessed be God for his infinite mercy in preserving us; I having gone
> through so much danger [. . .] escaping still myself, that I might live
> to recount & magnify his goodness to me.

Londoners welcomed the King, and according to one newspaper, the royal
return was:

> to the infinite Joy of this City, which they endeavoured to manifest, by
> Bells and Bonfires, and such other expressions and public rejoicings,
> as it is easy to imagine, for the Blessing they had so long wished for.

The Royal Society met again in the capital in March and by this time, the rest of the court had returned.[44]

Yet the plague was not over, Evelyn recording that, on 26 August, 'The contagion still continuing, we had church office [communion] at home'. In Deptford plague deaths only declined in October 1666.

Evelyn cannot have known that this plague was to be the last nationwide epidemic of bubonic plague. The reason for this was not – as some have suggested – because the brown rat replaced the black rat (the former can also carry plague), nor because Londoners developed immunity to the plague, nor because of the 'cleansing' effects of the Great Fire of London in 1666, but because the system of quarantine became more effective. Despite concerns in 1722 that a plague in France might cross the Channel, precautions were taken to ensure it never did. A terrible chapter had closed in London's history.[45]

The Fire of London 1666

Plague was not the only threat to London in the 1660s. Yet it was property, not people, that came under threat this time. Indeed, until the Blitz of 1940–1941, the Great Fire was the single most destructive event in London's history since its sack by Boudicca's forces in the first century. The fire began at a baker's shop in Pudding Lane at two in the morning of 2 September 1666 and lasted four days and nights. Among about 13,200 buildings destroyed were eighty-seven churches, forty-four livery halls and St Paul's Cathedral. Four-fifths of the city within the walls were reduced to ashes. The fire spread south to the Thames, east to the Tower of London, north as far as London Wall, and west almost as far as Chancery Lane. Fires, of course, were nothing new – Pepys recorded a number of fires occurring in London in the 1660s. But compared with the death toll wrought by the plague, very few died: perhaps only nine in all. Burnet exaggerated when he wrote: 'But what is a very miraculous circumstance, amidst all this destruction and public confusion, no person was known either to be burnt or trodden to death.' But the point is still made.[46]

The warm summer of 1666 was followed by a dry autumn. What little fire-fighting equipment existed in London happened to be ineffective. There were no water pumps, but such was the drought that water levels were low anyway. Buckets, ladders and grappling irons (for pulling houses down to create a fire break) were maintained in a few churches and public buildings. There was no fire brigade at that time: a regrettable situation as buildings were mostly constructed of wood, so fire was a serious hazard. Furthermore, streets were narrow and there were many warehouses full of coal, oil, wines and brandy to provide fuel for the fire. Finally, adverse winds were on hand to fan the flames.

The fire began early on Sunday morning at the house of Thomas Farriner, a contractor supplying ships' biscuits. Bakeries contained a great deal of combustible material, as well as ovens. Although Farriner later claimed all was well when he retired to bed, next morning smoke was issuing from the oven and the household's members had to escape from an upper window. Unfortunately, their maidservant was fearful of the escape route and remained behind – the Great Fire's first casualty.

The initial reaction to the breaking news of the fire was to ignore it. When officials told the Lord Mayor, Sir Thomas Bludworth, he thought it was not worth bothering about and famously remarked, 'Pish! A woman might piss it out!' Others were no wiser. Pepys recorded a similar reaction. On being told by his maids about 'a great fire they saw in the City', he wrote:

> So I rose, and slipped on my nightgown and went to her window, and thought it to be on the backside of Mark Lane at the furthest; but being unused to such fires as followed, I thought it far enough off, and so went to bed again and to sleep. About 7 rose again to dress myself, and there looked out of the window and saw the fire not so much as it was, and further off.[47]

Even later that morning there were some who paid little heed to the fire. Francisco de Rapicani, an official serving the former Queen Christina of Sweden, was aware of the fire but didn't allow this to interfere with lunch. Having met with a companion, de Rapicani later wrote:

> At midday, he took me to a meal with some of his friends, where there was a fine company gathered, including some men and women from the City. They were (God forgive us!) quite cheerful for so perilous and sorry a time.[48]

Likewise, Pepys and his wife 'had an extraordinary good dinner, and [were] as merry as at this time we could be'.[49]

Yet, for those who lived in the part of the city affected by fire, there was fear and flight, which increased as the fire spread. Pepys recorded the scene:

> Everybody endeavouring to remove their goods, and flinging into the River or bringing them into lighters that lay off. Poor people staying in their houses as long as till the very fire touched them, and then running into boats or clambering down one pair of stair by the waterside to another.[50]

Some people only escaped with their lives, Taswell recording 'These had escaped from the fire scarce under any covering except that of a blanket'. Goods were also carried off in the streets, some by carts, some on people's backs. Sick people were carried away in their beds. Goods were placed in churches for safety. One such church was St Faith's, where goods were deposited and all possible avenues to these possessions blocked up. The booksellers who had previously plied their trade around St Paul's, had put their wares in the great crypt. According to Taswell, 'The people who lived contiguous to St Paul's Church, raised their expectations greatly concerning the absolute security of that place on account of the immense thickness of its walls and its situation [...] They filled it with all sorts of goods.' One woman even sheltered in the cathedral. Alas for all concerned, the cathedral burnt down and the anonymous woman and all the stored goods were destroyed. Others, such as Isaacke Houblon, had moved their possessions twice on the first day of the fire and thought they would have to move them yet again. Some, such as Sir William Batten and Sir William Penn, stored their friends' goods in their houses.[51]

The Swedish ambassador was concerned that the fire might reach Covent Garden, where he resided. He asked the King if the staff of the Swedish embassy might move to new quarters further removed from the fire and this was agreed to. The Swedish delegation assembled like a military formation. The men were 'as well armed as possible' and the Swedish delegation kept together. This was just as well, for they saw 'an angry mob [...] young and old, men and women, all together, running, riding, walking, shouting, cursing and praying – we could scarcely pass through them'.[52]

On the evening of 2 September, Pepys himself was concerned that his own property might be burnt. He and his family packed their goods, to be ready for speedy removal. Some of their goods were buried in the garden at night-time, while Pepys's money and iron chests were hidden in the cellar. His bags of gold, important papers and accounts were put in boxes ready for despatch. Sir William Batten ordered carts to come in from the countryside in order to transport Pepys's goods away. Pepys, in his nightgown, took a cart laden with his treasures to Bethnal Green, noting that many others were also transporting their valuables in such a manner. By such actions, Pepys was reassured, 'I am eased at my heart to have my treasure so well secured'.[53] Many others did so, and managed to save their possessions. Richard Stephens wrote that:

> I suppose my brother Broomefield may have preserved most of his chief goods, for I hear many have so done, whose houses were nearer the place when the fire began.[54]

Some profited by the fire. The Duke de Repas told Sir Robert Harley that 'All people have had a very great loss by it except porters, cartsmen, and beggars. I have seen given 5 pounds for a load of goods from Cheapside to

Westminster, and myself have given nine shillings to a porter for a burden.' Lady Hobart wrote 'all the carts within 10 miles around, and cars and drays run about night and day'. One estimate for hiring a cart was £20 per load (perhaps as much as £2,520 in modern reckoning), though most charges were far lower – £5 or £10. Dr Denton wrote 'Our movables are saved, but at a vast charge, £4 for every load to Kensington'. Nevertheless, carts became scarce – Lady Hobart, having her possessions crated up, had to ask Lady Glastock for carts, writing that she 'cannot get a cart for money'. Those who could not afford such prices had to carry what they could on their backs. Some carriers of others' goods took the opportunity to rob their erstwhile employers. Taswell wrote:

> certain persons, assuming the character of porters, but in reality nothing else but downright plunderers, came and offered their assistance in removing our goods: we accepted; but they so far availed themselves of our service as to steal goods to the value of £40 from us.[55]

There was also downright theft. Pepys recorded open looting taking place. On 6 September, he wrote:

> I saw good Butts of sugar broke open in the street, and people go and take handfuls out and put into beer and drink it.[56]

Other instances of theft were recorded. Windham Sandys wrote: 'the poorer, they minded nothing but pilfering.' Mary Fisher was accused of 'stealing and carrying away several quantities of Virginia tobacco out of Fenchurch Street and Mincing Lane in the time of the late dreadful fire'. Thomas Hoggeflesh, a cooper, was said to have been responsible for 'feloniously taking away out of a cellar belonging to Mr Coresllis [a] six quart cask of brandy'.[57]

In order to try to prevent theft an order was issued to the parish constables of the City on 3 September. They were required to stand guard at designated points with 100 fellow parishioners and thirty soldiers during the nights of the fire. To encourage them, each man was given a shilling and provided with food and drink.

In contrast to their attitude towards Londoners during the plague, people in villages around London acted in a kindly manner – after all, these refugees posed no health risk. Carts were brought in from villages to help remove goods, and coaches were then sent to remove their owners. Clarendon wrote: 'all the neighbour villages were filled with more people than they could contain, and more goods than they could find room for'.[58]

Some of those who fled London encamped in fields outside the capital, 'which, for many miles, were strewn with movables of all sorts and tents erected to shelter both people and what goods they could get away'. Some citizens found themselves as far afield as Highgate. These people were helped by the King, who ordered that food be brought out to them. Otherwise, they might have starved, as they had taken their valuables, rather than food and drink, with them. This temporary camp did not last more than a few days, for when the fire ceased, the people either found shelter in the villages around London or in those parts of the city that had not burnt, 'all kind of people expressing a marvellous charity towards those who appeared to be undone'.[59]

Attempts to control and extinguish the fire were at first ineffectual. Flight, not fight, was on most people's minds. Evelyn wrote:

> The conflagration was so universal, and the people so astonished, that from the beginning – I know not by what despondency or fate – they hardly stirred to quench it. There was nothing heard or seen but crying out and lamentation, and running about like distracted creatures.

He later wrote that until 5 September, many 'stood as men restrained with their arms crossed'. Likewise, John Rushworth noted that 'when Cheapside was on fire, not ten men stood by helping or calling for help, I have been an eyewitness and can verify this and 100 times more'. Many people were so surprised at the fire's speed they were unable to save any of their goods, but only just escaped with their lives.[60]

Observers were shocked at the spectacle of the burning city which lay before their eyes. Evelyn wrote:

> O the miserable and calamitous spectacle, such as perhaps the whole world had not seen its like since the foundation of it: nor is it to be outdone until the world's universal conflagration. All the sky was of a fiery aspect like the top of a burning oven, and the light was seen above 40 miles round about for many nights. God grant my eyes may never behold the like [. . .] a resemblance of Sodom, or the Last Day. London was, but is no more.[61]

Evelyn took a coach after dinner on 2 September and went with his wife and son to the Thameside at Southwark and 'beheld that dismal spectacle'.[62] Rapicani echoed Evelyn's observations:

> At night it was really terrible to watch, for the whole air above the city seemed to be ablaze. The Thames looked like nothing so much

as a sheet of flame; in Thames Street as all the tar and fat and ship's stores had been thrown bodily into the river, then burning beams had come from the buildings that had been burnt or pulled down, setting it on fire, so that the sight was more awful than anything one could imagine.[63]

Pepys, however, made a decisive intervention. He saw the fire at first-hand, then took a boat down the Thames to Whitehall. After relating the news of the fire, he was summoned by the King himself. Pepys told him and his brother, the Duke of York, 'unless His Majesty did command houses to be pulled down, nothing could stop the fire'. Apparently the fire 'affected His Majesty with [...] tenderness and compassion' and he visited the scene, declaring that 'all possible means should be used for quenching the fires or stopping its further spreading'. Charles II also appointed Pepys as his intermediary with Bludworth (a man whom Pepys already had a low opinion of), with orders to have the Lord Mayor pull houses down. Soldiers were promised, too, to help with the task of demolition.[64] Pepys met Bludworth in Canning Street. The latter was

> like a man spent, with a handkerchief about his neck [...] he cried like a fainting woman 'Lord what can I do? I am spent. People will not obey me. I have been pulling down houses. But the fire overtakes us faster than we can do it.'

Bludworth, though he had initially ignored the fire, had risen in the early hours in order to try, however ineffectually, to control it. A chain of men tried to use buckets of water to combat the flames but this was inadequate and the fire spread still further. This had the effect of disheartening others beside the Lord Mayor. Clarendon wrote: 'all men stood amazed as spectators only, no man knowing what remedy to apply, nor the magistrates what orders to give'.[65] Bludworth has been much criticised for his inability to cope in this moment of supreme crisis, but he was no worse than others, as Clarendon observed:

> yet having never been used to such spectacles, his consternation was equal to that of other men, nor did he know how to apply his authority to the remedying of the present distress.[66]

It had been suggested by some sailors, that if enough houses were mined with gunpowder and blown up, there would be a space between the flames and the remaining houses. This idea was not adopted because various aldermen did not want to see their own property destroyed in such a manner. Bludworth felt he could not order the destruction of property without the owners' consent. He would have been acting illegally in doing so, in any case, and would have to reimburse the cost. In any case, fires in London were frequent and Bludworth thought the fire would not be serious. Furthermore, due to the season, many wealthy men and their families had quit town for the country. They had no one to help them; indeed in some cases, even when wealthy absentees had friends nearby, the latter felt they could not break into their absent friends' houses in order to rescue precious possessions because, in doing so, they would be committing a felony.

One small step that was taken against part of the fire occurred on 3 September. John Dolben, Dean of Westminster, led the Westminster schoolboys to fight the blaze. Taswell recorded: 'We were employed many hours in fetching water from the backside of St Dunstan's in the East, where we happily extinguished the fire.'[67]

The fire was not the only danger then prevalent in the capital. According to Clarendon, just as the flames were at their height,

> all of which kindled another fire in the breasts of men, almost as dangerous as that within their houses [...] Monday morning produced first a jealousy, and then a universal conclusion, that this fire came not by chance [...] [but] [...] by conspiracy and combination.

Those suspected were Frenchmen (in January 1666 France had joined Holland in its war against England) and any Dutch then in London. According to Taswell:

> A blacksmith, in my presence, meeting an innocent Frenchman walking down the street, felled him instantly to the ground with an iron bar.

It did not matter that many of these men had lived in London for many years and were hitherto considered respectable citizens. Frightened men wanted scapegoats and these foreigners seemed to fit the bill. Some even believed stories that an armed host of Frenchmen were marching on London.[68] Consequently, foreigners – and later, Catholics – were assaulted, both verbally and physically. Rapicani noted the 'atrocities the maddened people were committing against foreigners'. Some laid low to escape such suffering, others were arrested and gaoled for their own safety, not because they were suspected by those in authority. Houses belonging to Frenchmen were searched and when fire-works were found in some, the suspicions of the searchers seemed justified. Taswell recorded how 'the incensed populace, divesting a French painter of all the goods in his shop, then levelled his house', believing that, otherwise, the

Frenchman would have burnt it in order to start another conflagration. The only consolation was that:

> in this general rage of the people no mischief was done to the strangers, that no one of them was assassinated outright, though many were sorely beaten and bruised.

The King sent messages around London to try to prevent such assaults. Militia and soldiers patrolled the streets to foil further outrages against foreigners.[69]

Two lords saw a servant of the Portuguese ambassador attacked in the street. Knowing little English, he was unable to speak in his own defence. Fortunately, however, the poor man was rescued from his tormentors. He was alleged to have put his hand into his pocket and thrown a fireball into a building, which then caught fire. But the truth of the matter was that the hapless servant had seen a piece of bread on the ground, which he put in his pocket before depositing it in the first house he came across – apparently, an old Portuguese custom. The piece of bread was found exactly where he claimed it would be. The man was retained in custody, however, and was given a mock interrogation before being released. Likewise, Taswell's brother saw a Frenchman molested because it was thought that the chest he was carrying contained fireballs. These turned out to be tennis balls.

It was not just 'the ignorant and deluded mob' – to quote Taswell – who believed that foreigners were to blame. Lady Hobart wrote of the origins of the fire: 'it did begin in Pudding Lane at a baker's, where a Dutch rogue lay [. . .] Tis the Dutch fire'.[70]

It was not until 4 September that effectual steps were taken to fight the flames. Houses in Tower Street, next to the Tower of London, were blown up (frightening those who heard the explosion) and what little flames remained were easily quenched. Fire engines were ordered up from Deptford and Woolwich.

There was more action on the following day, after which the fire was eventually extinguished. More houses were blown up. The wind abated, which helped. Despite further despair, the courage and industry of those fighting the fires prevailed. Some of those who were helping to stop the fire were the workmen at the royal dockyards of Deptford and Woolwich, whose employment Pepys had advocated. The demolition of houses created a break between combustible wooden buildings and the fire. By the end of Wednesday, 5 September, the fire was all but over, being finally extinguished the following morning. The main reason for this was a change in the wind's direction, as well as a drop in its strength: without this, all the efforts of the firefighters would have been in vain.

If the King had shown little spirit during the Great Plague (by quitting the capital), he showed a different side to his character during the Great Fire. Burnet wrote:

> The King and the Duke [of York], with the Guards, were almost all the day on horseback, seeing to all that could be done, either for quenching the fire or for carrying off persons and goods to the fields. The King was never observed to be so much struck with anything in his life.[71]

Clarendon echoed this, writing:

> The pains the King had taken day and night during the fire, and the dangers he had exposed himself to, even for the saving of the citizens' goods had been very notorious.

Charles's actions impressed his subjects. The Duke of York also won praise, John Rushworth writing that he:

> hath won the hearts of the people with his continual and indefatigable pains day and night in helping quench the fire, handing buckets of water with as much diligence as the poorest man that did assist; if the Lord Mayor had done as much his example might have gone far towards saving the city.[72]

Some, including privy councillors, thought that the fire was no accident and had been caused by human hands. According to Burnet:

> The question was then and is still a secret, whether the fire came casually or on design; and however the general opinion might be that it was casual, yet there are some presumptions on the other side of a very odd nature.

However, one Robert Hubert – a French Protestant accused of being Catholic – confessed to starting the fire and was duly hanged at Tyburn, despite the fact that he was insane and no proof of his guilt was forthcoming. Other suspects included Dutchmen and Republicans. Charles did his best to quell such suspicions and had a committee appointed by Parliament to investigate the matter. Without a shred of credible proof to the contrary, the committee concluded the fire was accidental. Nevertheless, many foreigners opted to quit the country when the opportunity arose.[73]

But it was not only foreigners who were blamed in the aftermath of the fire. It was claimed that John Hobbes did

> wilfully and maliciously set fire to his own house, by the burning of which house he wilfully and feloniously set fire to the adjoining dwelling house of George Grimes and by fire destroyed the same.

Meanwhile, Elizabeth Shaw was accused of possessing a stock of fireballs and other combustibles with ill intent. Both were found not guilty.[74]

A more realistic estimation was made by one John Rushworth:

> Let us not lay the fault upon the French or Dutch, or our own people for throwing Fireballs, &c., for by all I can observe it was *digitans dei* [by the hand of God].[75]

But some people remained upbeat. Rapicani had no reason to love the English, as mobs had threatened him and his fellows, yet he wrote the following tribute to the bravery of the English:

> It was indeed a pitiful sight, but the people's courage was so resilient, for the English are by nature not easily daunted, that it was not so much the loss caused by the dreadful fire that they were talking and worrying about, as the war that they were waging on the sea against the Dutch.[76]

In spite of the damage caused by the Great Fire, many bonfires were lit in London on 5 November. Yet this was probably an act of defiance, as 5 November marked the deliverance of the Protestant King and government from Catholic conspirators in 1605, and many believed in 1666 that the fire had been caused by Catholics. Thus the bonfires may be seen as an act of Protestant defiance in the face of real or imagined enemies.

Yet some were privately haunted by memories of the fire. Pepys recorded two dreams he had a few weeks after the conflagration. On 25 September, he wrote 'So home to bed – and all night still mightily troubled in my sleep with fire and houses pulling down'. Two days later he wrote: 'A very furious blowing all the night, and my mind still mightily perplexed with dreams and burning the rest of the town.' Beneath the surface of the apparent English calm lurked real anxieties.[77] In public, however, the people of London implored God's forgiveness. On 10 October, Evelyn wrote:

> This day was indicted a General Fast through the nation, to humble us, upon the late dreadful conflagration, added to the plague & war, the most dismal judgements could be inflicted, & indeed but what we

highly deserved for our prodigious ingratitude, burning lusts, dissolute court, profane & abominable lives, under such dispensations of God's continued favour, in restoring Church, prince & people from our late intestine calamities.

Churches in London were well attended on this day, as Pepys recorded. He went to St Margaret's, Westminster, where 'it was so full, no standing there' and later that day he went to another church, 'but the crowd so great'. Yet life went on, with Pepys writing that, at Islington, 'Here eat and drank and merry'.[78]

Turning to practical matters, the City was rebuilt in the following years. Evelyn wrote:

> I presented his Majesty with a Survey of the ruins, and a Plot for a new City, with a discourse on it, whereupon, after dinner His Majesty sent for me into the Queen's bedchamber, her Majesty and the Duke [of York] only present, where they examined each particular, & discoursed upon them for near a full hour, seeming to be extremely pleased with what I had thought early on.[79]

Yet the initial grandiose and expensive plans devised by Evelyn and others to create a new baroque city came to nothing. Property rights were sacrosanct and speedy rebuilding was required, in order that business could resume as soon as possible. Christopher Wren played a prominent part, designing many of the City churches, as well as the Monument that commemorates the fire, and, of course, St Paul's Cathedral. Ironically, only days before the fire, Evelyn and Wren had been discussing the rebuilding of the cathedral anyway. Perhaps most importantly, the new City was made of brick and stone, helping ensure that a fire would never again cause so much damage. Thus the medieval city was erased and the modern city arrived.

Another result of the fire was that civic fire-fighting methods were improved, both in London and in other cities and towns in England – the Great Fire acting as a wake-up call. Furthermore, insurance companies sprang up in London, each with its own fire engine and crew – but only for the protection of those customers who paid their insurance premiums.

Over the next two decades it was not natural disasters but political and religious issues that threatened London – the chief concern being who would succeed Charles II as king. Charles had no legitimate children and his brother James, Duke of York, was next in line. But James was a zealous convert to Catholicism, which did not go down well with the population at large. Unsurprisingly – given the extent of anti-Catholic hysteria – concerted attempts were made to prevent James's accession. To this end, in 1678, Titus Oates spread stories about a Catholic plot, which were initially believed. In fact, Oates reminded his audience that the Catholics had been 'responsible' for the Great Fire. Consequently, some Catholics were arrested and several executed. Yet despite all this, Oates was discredited and James succeeded his brother as king in 1685.

Anti-Catholic Riots 1688

Over the next three years James's policies aimed at abolishing the existing penal laws against Catholics and, as part of this programme, he appointed Catholics to positions of power – something unheard-of since the previous century. Catholics could now worship openly, thanks to James. From the standpoint of the early twenty-first century, this may appear a laudable policy. The problem was that it went against all the prejudices of the vast bulk of the nation, which was about 99 per cent Protestant: divided as they were on other issues, Britons were united in their anti-Catholicism. Catholicism was seen as akin to tyranny and, in any case, was linked with hostile foreign powers, notably France and Spain. James II's actions, although aimed at making life more tolerable for England's Catholics, actually made them worse by galvanising all who feared and hated Catholicism.

In 1688, the birth of a legitimate male heir to James's Queen raised the prospect of a long line of Catholic monarchs. Unwilling to countenance this, a group of dissident nobles, led by William Russell, asked William of Orange (the newly appointed 'stadholder' of the Netherlands, who, in 1677 had married James's daughter Mary, making him the English monarch's son-in-law) to lead an army to England, in order to defend the Protestant cause. William did so in November, and although James intended to oppose him by force, he fell victim to panic and abandoned the idea. On 11 December James quit the capital in an attempt to flee to France, leaving his co-religionists without their royal protector – seemingly all-powerful until William's intervention. London was now left without its 'chief magistrate'. Furthermore, there was an invading army approaching while a leaderless British Army was in the process of collapse. Reliable news was limited and rumours were rife. Some Londoners thought the capital's Catholics might be dangerous; that Irishmen in the British Army might join them in order to assist James. The Protestant mob decided to act first, launching a spate of attacks Catholic properties in the metropolis. As in 1554 and 1661, religion played a large part in deciding men's actions: yet there was no evidence of any Catholic plot and, in fact, the Catholic minority was isolated and afraid.

Roger Morrice, a prosperous Londoner, made the following observation regarding the dangerous situation he witnessed:

> The mob was up in most parts of the town all Tuesday night and committed many tumultuous insolences, and made the same invasion upon liberty and property, to the great grief of all wise men and to the great scandal of the City.[80]

Evelyn, in his diary, wrote with similar concern:

> The rabble people demolish all papists' chapels and several popish lords' and gentlemen's houses – especially that of the Spanish ambassador, which they pillaged, and burnt his library.[81]

What is notable is that both these observers were Protestants and ordinarily unsympathetic towards the Catholic cause. But attacks by the lower orders on property was another matter – one that united all property owners. Moreover, who could tell what might happen next, where it would end?

The rioters – described by Burnet as 'the apprentices and rabble' – had gathered in the streets on the evening of Tuesday 11 December. An anonymous man was chosen as leader. A contemporary journal announced: 'No sooner was the King's withdrawing known, but the Mob consulted to wreak their Vengeance on Papists and Popery.' This is the first occasion the term 'mob' is known to have been used; some used the term 'Mobile' instead. They had attacked chapels belonging to ambassadors of Catholic countries and public mass houses, including those at Lincoln Field's Inn, Lime Street and one near the Archway. Timber and furniture from these places was taken away and some of it burnt. Even bricks were carried away – a valuable commodity in those times. The violence and the damage was extensive – Morrice wrote 'I think few Popish ambassadors' chapels [. . .] have escaped'.[82]

One exception was that of the French ambassador, but that was because he had always paid his debts promptly to the tradesmen he dealt with – in contrast to his opposite number at the Spanish embassy, who did not, and whose property, as Evelyn noted, was singled out as a target. The French and Venetian ambassadors had taken the wise precaution of asking for troops to deter the rioters. That of Spain did not, thinking his country's great standing would deter the mob. A Catholic printing press was also attacked and destroyed. Terror was a common reaction, even among Protestants. One observer wrote: 'This night I was frightened with the wonderful light in the sky' when the chapel in Lincoln Field's Inn was burnt. Not since the Great Fire of 1666 had London been ablaze to such an extent.[83]

There are no reports of any London Catholics being physically attacked – probably because they had fled or were in hiding. Evelyn noted that 'The papists in offices lay down their commissions and fly – universal consternation amongst them'. Another observer wrote that the Catholics spent the day:

> running into all holes to hide themselves, weeping and crying for fear
> of their lives and all their temporal interest, carrying their goods
> away in bundles to one Protestant's house, and then to another, and
> very few durst receive them.

No resistance was ever offered when the rioters broke into chapels. Even the dowager Queen, Catherine of Braganza, would not shelter fellow Catholics at Somerset House, as she feared it might provoke an attack by the mob. One woman, who had seven Catholic lodgers in her house was 'up all night for fear of the Mob'.[84]

Some Catholics also tried to save their possessions as well as their lives. Richer ones placed their plate, jewellery and money at the Spanish ambassador's house. One woman deposited £800 in a case there (almost £70,000 in modern terms). All was lost when the ambassador's residence was destroyed and the goods inside either stolen or burnt. Others, though, were luckier, as a contemporary newspaper noted: 'many Loads of Papists' Goods were removed at the other end of the Town, to avoid the hands of the Spoilers'. Elsewhere, discretion was called for. Publicans and shopkeepers whose premises bore Catholic names – such as Cardinal's Cap, The Nun's Head and The Pope's Head – removed these signs lest they offended the mob.[85]

Such lawlessness was not confined to Tuesday, 11 December, but continued the following day on the report of a disturbing rumour. Morrice wrote: 'And then universal terrible alarm was taken all over London and Westminster with a fear and confident persuasion, that they should have their throats cut by the French and by the Papists.' On the next day, there was an additional rumour to this, 'that the disbanded Irish, who were thereby provoked, would join with the English Papists to cut all their throats'.[86]

Meanwhile, what of the authorities, whose principal task was to keep London in a state of peace and order? Many did not have tender feelings towards Catholics or James II. A convention of senior politicians and magistrates met on 11 December, on learning of James's departure and of William's possible arrival. The Earl of Craven, Lord Lieutenant of Middlesex, was asked to summon the London and Middlesex militia 'for preventing any disorders which might happen in the suburbs of London'. He told the convention this order had already been given, so no more thought was given to the matter. The convention then went on to discuss the other dangers facing the capital – one being that the troops in the capital might come into conflict with those of the approaching William. They ordered James's disbanded and demoralised army from London. This directive may seem to contradict the one concerning the militia, but, while the latter force remained under the convention's direct control, regular forces might have retained their former allegiance to James and fought his enemies. Meanwhile, orders were issued to disarm all Catholics, adding fuel to the public perception of them as dangerous fanatics and raising panic levels even higher.[87]

Although the militia had been summoned and were under arms in London on the night of 11 December, their performance was variable. Some do not appear to have interfered with the activities of the mobs. This was probably because, as fellow Protestants, they sympathised with their co-religionists, seeing Catholics as the greater enemy and the rioters as allies. Yet another source claims that it was inability to act, not disinclination: 'The militia of London and Westminster were immediately up in arms. They could not prevent the mob from assembling and committing some disorders.' Yet they did deter attacks on Catholic property in the City. When one Captain Douglas ordered his men to fire on the rioters, he was shot by his own men – perhaps by accident, but perhaps not. This action would hardly encourage other officers to act with necessary firmness.[88]

Yet, on the following morning (12 December), the scenes of devastation were clear for all to see. The attacks on foreign embassies caused particular concern to the convention, which was concerned about Britain's international standing. Ambassadorial property was thought to be sacrosanct and under the protection of the host government. Official apologies were sent to all ambassadors and especially that of Spain. They were told that compensation would be given and that protection would be offered. One observer noted: 'All sober people are extraordinarily concerned at this horrid violation of the law of nations.'[89]

Although the provisional government had been caught unawares by the scale of the violence on 11 December, it would not allow this to happen again. Orders were passed and then printed for distribution, announcing that no one should pull down Catholic chapels. The sheriffs of London, Middlesex and Surrey, along with the Justices of the Peace, deputy lieutenants and constables, were to 'execute their offices, making use of the militia and the *posse comitatus* to suppress riots which cannot be suppressed by the civil officers'. As an even sterner threat, twenty-two cannon were brought to the Tower of London in case their use was necessary. The Regiment of Foot Guards was also summoned to help keep order. They were even allowed to open fire if need be.[90] Such threats were essential. Nicholas Luttrell wrote:

> They would have plundered and demolisht the houses of several papists, as the Lord Powys, the late Judge Alllibons &c., if they had not been prevented by the Trained Bands which were out; a party of Horse were also out who did at last disperse them.[91]

Only the deployment of reliable troops and strict orders that they prevent future disorder was successful. Units of cavalry, infantry and artillery were positioned throughout London. The people may also have become calmer when they heard that William of Orange had been officially invited to London by the City. Certainly, the mob was reported to have been 'crying out they should not go till the Prince of Orange came to Town', but otherwise not acting in a violent fashion. The rioting was over, but it had been a violent night.[92]

William and his wife Mary were crowned as William III and Mary II the following year. All James's policies in favour of Catholics were now at an end and anti-Catholic laws were enacted by Parliament. Anti-Catholicism was to be a tool of government for the next century and nothing was done to excite the anti-Catholic prejudices of the masses until the later eighteenth century, as we shall see in the following chapter.

Conclusion

The seventeenth century had been one of the worst in Britain's history. Many of the crises had centred on London. Londoners had reacted in a number of ways to the plague and fire. In the case of the former, some fled but many remained at their posts – though for a variety of reasons. Some, perhaps in desperation, turned to crime. During the Great Fire, flight and the safe-guarding of moveable property were foremost. Again, the dark side of human nature showed itself as foreigners were made scapegoats and some assaulted in the streets. Thefts rose, yet social order did not collapse.

Despite the two great tragedies of 1665–1666, London recovered. Its population, as ever swelled by immigration from the rest of the British Isles, continued to grow. By 1700 the capital's population was at least half a million, whereas, on the eve of the plague, the figure had been about 400,000. After all, although the loss in life had been significant, the majority had survived. Rebuilding after the fire was rapid and by the following decade a new city had come into being. Business thrived and trade rose once more. Wren, whose cathedral was finished in 1710, wrote:

however disastrous it might be to the then inhabitants, had prov'd infinitely beneficent to their posterity; conducting vastly to the Riches and opulency [*sic*], as of the splendour of the City.[93]

The Great Plague and the Great Fire had been tragic but they did not have any long-term negative effects. Life went on, though the memories of catastrophe lived on, too. Compared with these, the Venner Revolt of 1661 and the anti-Catholic riots of almost three decades later, may seem less dramatic. These were short-lived crises, but they caused great fear among Londoners. In the former, a minority had terrorised the majority; in the latter, it was the other way around. Similar behaviour was to be repeated in London's later history.

Chapter 3

The Eighteenth and Nineteenth Centuries 1715–1887

One might see the glare of the conflagration fill the sky from many parts. The sight was dreadful.[1]

Rioting was an irregular feature of life in London in the eighteenth and nineteenth centuries. Some riots were aimed at those in authority, with unpopular laws being opposed – such as the Gin Act and the Excise Bill in the eighteenth century – or in favour of political reform in the nineteenth. Some political marches for reform, however, have turned violent and clashes with the police occasionally occurred in the nineteenth century. Unpopular minorities were also in danger from rioters – often Catholics and Protestant Dissenters found themselves in danger. This chapter deals with a small selection of these civil disturbances.

First of all, the legal definition of a riot is as follows:

> A tumultuous disturbance of the peace by three persons or more, who assemble together of their own authority, with an intent mutually to assist one another against anyone who shall oppose them in the execution of an enterprise of a private nature, and afterwards actually execute the enterprise, in a violent and turbulent manner, to the terror of the people, whether the act intended were lawful or unlawful.[2]

Although there have been many laws passed against riots, they became much sterner with the passing of the Riot Act in 1715. This enabled a magistrate to read the Act before a group of a dozen or more, and if they did not disperse within an hour, force – whether civil or military – could be used to make them do so. The destruction of property also became a crime. But apart from these various riots, there were even more dangerous events. One was the threat, in 1745, posed by the last hostile army to march on London. Yet, if these centuries marked the end of an old threat, they also witnessed the advent of a new danger – terrorist bombings.

The Jacobite Riots 1715

William III died in 1702 and was replaced by his sister-in-law, Anne – the last of the Stuarts to reign. With no surviving children on her death in 1714, George I became the new king. He was a German – the first of the Hanoverian monarchs – his great virtue was that he was a Protestant, his rivals being Catholic and so excluded from the succession.

In London his coronation had gone smoothly. This was despite the fact that there was an alternative monarch, the Catholic James Francis Stuart (son of James II, who had died in 1701), who also claimed the throne. His supporters were known as Jacobites, after Jacobus, the Latin for James. Some Tories and High Churchmen were sympathetic towards James – who, they hoped, might convert to Protestantism – recognising him as the legitimate hereditary monarch by right of blood. Jacobite support is hard to estimate accurately, but by 1715 hostility towards King George – and his supporters, the Whigs and the Dissenters, the former making up the King's new government – was clearly apparent. Indeed, suspicion of the new foreign King and his allies erupted violently on the streets of London on a number of occasions in that year (as it did elsewhere throughout the country). Economic dislocation following the end of the War of Spanish Succession and the subsequent disbanding of soldiers and sailors also resulted in discontent, and these 'Jacobite' riots were a way in which these grievances could be vented.

For once, anti-Catholicism was not a factor in the riots, although there was a religious dimension. George I had publicly identified his interests with the Dissenters, despite the fact that they were loathed by the majority, as demonstrated in 1710 when Dissenting chapels were attacked by the London mob. Thus, George and his government were assailed on several counts: political, economic and religious.

The first of these riots occurred on 23 April 1715, the birthday of the preceding monarch, the esteemed Queen Anne. The second occurred on 28 May, the birthday of King George. The third occurred on 29 May, anniversary of the restoration of Charles II in 1660. Finally, there was a clash between Jacobite and Loyalist mobs on 17 November.

On all these occasions, large numbers of people took to the London streets to show their hostility to the new order and their respect for the Stuart monarchs past and, they hoped, future. They also attacked the supporters of the new order, both their persons and their property. Some Whigs thought there was a dark conspiracy behind these demonstrations, inspired and funded by Tory and Jacobite clergymen and gentry, claiming, 'the Faction who has been at pains and expense some time before to prepare a rascally mob employed their tools to assemble them'. There is, however, no direct evidence for this.[3]

On 23 April the mob hung up a flag and a hoop on Snow Hill. Allegedly, they had been provided with money to buy wine and build a bonfire to light up the night. They also erected a picture of the late Queen. They then marched through London, intimidating others. Householders were encouraged to put candles in their windows in order to show their support and to shout 'God bless the Queen and the High Church!' Some did so willingly, others through fear. Some were 'persuaded' to give money to the mob. Those who did not had their windows broken. A pregnant woman and a servant maid were injured by stones. Dissenting chapels were threatened with destruction – and as this had occurred in 1710, the threats were not empty.[4]

A contemporary historian, Peter Rae, remarked of the disorders of 29 May, 'The Mobs in the City broke the Windows of such Houses as were not illuminated, and those of the Lord Mayor amongst them: Their cry was High Church and Ormond [a leading Jacobite].' At Smithfield, a picture of William III – hero of the Whigs – was publicly burnt. A French Catholic priest proclaimed that King George had no right to the throne. The windows of a Dissenting chapel were removed and the bell ropes of another church were cut so they could not ring for George I. Constables and watchmen were attacked.[5] A newspaper sympathetic to the King's cause noted the ineffectual behaviour of those responsible for order in April:

> it were to be wished that our officers of the Peace did exert themselves of their own accord, on such occasions, for when people are suddenly attacked by such numerous Mobs [. . .] they cannot well have an opportunity of sending for constables &c., and in such cases, the Justices and constables of the neighbourhood, who have a power to disperse such rascals, can never be supposed to want due notice of it.

There was only a little resistance – a constable asked the rioters to desist but was disregarded and insulted for his trouble.[6]

Yet the mobs did not always have their own way. On 29 May, although there were no forces on hand to suppress the rioters at once, time allowed those opposed to the rioters to gather. Some citizens and constables congregated at Cheapside and managed to arrest thirty of their enemy. The Jacobite Catholic priest was arrested, tried and eventually flogged for his seditious cries.

Unlike the disturbances of 1688, there were some who did not condemn the rioters for their destructive acts. The Whiggish Dudley Ryder (1689–1757), a law student, recounted a conversation with the Marshall family in June 1715. They denied that the riots were the work of the Tories, claiming that the Whigs were responsible. Ryder, however, blamed the London glaziers for breaking windows in order to drum up trade, adding that 'the Tories suffered equally with the Whigs'.

Some did not even record their happening, and Lady Cowper, wife of the Lord Chancellor, did not even refer to the riots in her diary of this period.[7]

The rioters were not the 'apprentices' and 'rabble' accused of rioting in 1688. They were, in fact – judging by those put on trial afterwards – a cross-section of society. They included shopkeepers, craftsmen and labourers, with even a few professional men and gentlemen. In the autumn of 1715, Jacobite armies were formed in Scotland and northern England, and these rebellions were serious indeed.

It was on 17 November that the final Jacobite riot of 1715 took place. There was a Loyalist Society – probably financed by government supporters such as the young Duke of Newcastle. The Society was based at the Roebuck Inn on Cheapside and its members planned to meet on the 17th, in order to celebrate the anniversary of the accession of Queen Elizabeth I and the defeat of the Jacobite army at Preston on 14 November 1715. Loyal toasts would be drunk – especially to George I. But the Loyalists heard that a Jacobite mob planned to burn effigies of their heroes – William III, George I and the Duke of Marlborough – at Smithfield. These effigies were being stored in a house in Aldersgate. The Loyalists marched to the house and took the effigies, with a Jacobite found there, who was taken prisoner. In the evening, the Jacobite mob of about 500 men came to the Roebuck in search of their effigies. They shouted 'High Church and Ormonde, High Church and the King, High Church and the Church of Rome!' They began to threaten the Loyalists inside the Roebuck and then began to stone the windows, pulling down the inn's sign and declaring they would destroy the whole building.[8]

Although outnumbered, the Loyalists inside the Roebuck were not cowering. They told their enemies to desist, which they did not. Then they filled their muskets with powder – but not ball – and fired. Again, this had no effect. Finally, the Loyalists loaded their guns with live ammunition and fired. Two of the attackers were killed and several were injured. Even so, the riot did not end. Then the Lord Mayor, assisted by officers and citizens shouting 'King George forever!' arrived and arrested some of the crowd, the rest escaping into the night.[9]

There were further riots in the following year, but these were the last Jacobite riots in London. They probably petered out because the Jacobite rebellion of 1715 had failed and the forces of law and order had gained the upper hand. It is noteworthy that there were no Jacobite riots in London at the time of the final Jacobite rebellion of 1745. Yet some leading politicians did see the hand of Jacobitism in other riots that took place in the capital in the

1730s. These were aimed at the government's unpopular policies, such as the Excise Bill and the Gin Act, or against Irishmen who undercut local wages. Yet none threatened the monarchy and government themselves.

The Jacobite Invasion 1745

In 1745 James Francis Stuart was too old for any further adventures. His son, Charles Edward Stuart – also known as Bonnie Prince Charlie – was not. He made what was to be the last serious Jacobite attempt to regain the throne in 1745. His Jacobite army, composed of Scots, marched south in an attempt to reach London. This force had reached Derby by early December, only about 123 miles from London, having outmarched two opposing armies, one of which was led by the King's son, the Duke of Cumberland. It seemed that the next step was about to be taken towards the capital. So far, all resistance to the Jacobites had been ineffectual.

There has been much discussion among historians about the state of London at this critical time. Some allege the capital was in a state of panic: some later referring to 6 December, the day Londoners learnt of the progress of the Jacobite army, as 'Black Friday'. Alternatively, it has been argued that London was enthusiastically in favour of the Jacobite cause. Others argue that support for the established monarchy of George II was strong and panic was minimal. The Chevalier de Johnstone, a Jacobite officer, later wrote in his memoirs:

> The whole city [...] was filled with terror and consternation. Many of the inhabitants fled to the country with their most precious effects, and all the shops were shut. People thronged to the Bank to obtain payment of its notes, and it only escaped bankruptcy by a stratagem [...] King George ordered his yachts, in which he had embarked all his most precious effects, to remain at the Tower quay, in readiness to sail at a moment's notice [...] the Duke of Newcastle [a leading politician] [...] remained inaccessible in his own house the whole of 6th of December, weighing in his mind the part which it would be most prudent to take, and even uncertain whether he should immediately declare for the Pretender [Charles Edward Stuart]. It was even said that in London, that fifty thousand men had actually left that city to meet the Prince and join his army.[10]

Similarly, another Jacobite officer claimed: 'it is probable that when we approached that great city many people would also have joined us; I hear there were 30 thousand ready to do so.' Yet neither man was in London at the time and could not know how far the rumours they had picked up were true.[11] Certainly, there is some contemporary evidence that supports these views,

not least from the anti-Jacobite periodical, the *True Patriot*, edited by Henry
Fielding (1707–1754), a London novelist and journalist:

> On Friday last, the alarm of the rebels having given the Duke
> [of Cumberland] the slip, and being in full march for the town, with
> the Express above mentioned from Admiral Vernon [that there was
> a French invasion fleet in readiness to sail] struck such a Terror into
> several public-spirited persons, that to prevent their money, jewels,
> plate, etc., falling into rebellious or French hands, they immediately
> began to pack up and secure the same. And that they themselves
> might not be forced against their will into that company, they began
> to prepare for journeys into the country.[12]

Responses in the capital varied throughout the period of the rebellion. At the
end of August there was concern among the Whig elite. The Lord Chancellor,
Hardwicke, wrote to Thomas Herring, Archbishop of York, on the 31st: 'There
seems to be a certain indifference and deadness amongst many and the Spirit
of the Nation wants to be roused and animated.' Horace Walpole, man of
letters and son of the late premier, wrote six days later: 'The Confusion I have
found and the danger we are in, prevent me talking of anything else.' Yet, on
7 September, he reported a sense of apathy:

> I have found everyone in – I was going to say confusion – but I can't
> say that [...] everyone seems as much unconcerned as if it was
> only some Indian king brought over by Oglethorpe [General James
> Oglethorpe, founder of the colony of Georgia].[13]

According to Lady Hardwicke, the Jacobites spread a story that Newcastle and
his brother, Henry Pelham, First Lord of the Treasury, had fled to join them
and 'as ridiculous and false as these reports may seem, they gain'd a universal
run, and were propagated with uncommon address'. Only when Newcastle
showed himself to the crowd of concerned Londoners did the rumour dissipate.
Such attitudes can be partly explained by the fact that few regular troops were
in England until late September, and by the fact that many of the elite took *any*
opposition to the government for latent Jacobitism. As Newcastle wrote to the
Duke of Cumberland, the King's third son and Captain-General:

> For, had not the reinforcement [ten battalions] providentially arrived,
> the day before the news of Sir John Cope's defeat [at Prestonpans]
> the confusion in the city of London would not have been to be
> described.[14]

But on 4 October Walpole could confidently write: 'The good people of England have at last rubbed their eyes and looked about them, a wonderful spirit is risen in all counties among all sorts of people.' John Tucker, a Dorset MP who was in London, noted:

> There seems to be a general spirit all over the Nation to rise against this Pretender and I hope it will increase to such a Degree as to frighten him back.[15]

When the Jacobites reached Derby on 4 December, there was a mixture of consternation and steadfastness among Londoners. Hardwicke feared that a strong body of regular troops was needed to defend the capital 'to procure some Quiet to the Minds of the people here and prevent that prodigious harm and confusion, which otherwise would distract this capital and affect all commerce and credit.' One of his sons, Joseph Yorke, wrote: 'The motion of the rebels to Derby threw us into no small panic here.' On 14 December Tucker reflected: 'this good city was in the utmost consternation from the apprehension of the arrival of the Highland army.' Walpole's assessment was mixed, observing that the rebels put 'the town into great consternation', while adding, 'in London the aversion to them is amazing'.[16]

Another sign of fear is that the financial markets were shaky. Bank stock stood at 143 in early September 1745; when the Jacobites were at Derby it was 131, not recovering until the end of December, when the Jacobites were in retreat. Tucker observed – just after the news of the Jacobite victory of Prestonpans had reached the capital – 'public credit is greatly affected, the stocks sink and some people seem to be much dejected'. Yet the run on the Bank, as recounted by Johnstone, occurred in September, and had been successfully resolved soon after. According to the Reverend Thomas Birch, writing on 14 September, 'some persons have been silently disengaging themselves from the Funds'. Two weeks later, he wrote that the 'ill-affected' had been crowding the Bank. According to Lady Hardwicke, the panic had been initiated by two Scottish bankers, presumably in an effort to disrupt credit and weaken the financial sinews of the state.[17]

As befitted the commercial and financial hub of Britain, support from the merchants was forthcoming. One commentator noted: 'the city is giving great marks of their zeal and loyalty'. An address of loyalty was conveyed to the King on 11 September by merchants in 160 coaches – indicative of the high level of mercantile support. They also acted practically. On 26 September, a number of merchants met at Garraway's coffee house to discuss how they might support public credit. They decided that they would not refuse bank notes in payment. At least 1,140 merchants signed up to this scheme. This resulted in stopping the run of creditors on the Bank of England, where the directors had made payments in silver, not gold, in order to delay the running down of specie. Hardwicke strongly approved of this action: 'Your Grace sees by the printed papers what has been done by the merchants of London to support the Bank and thereby public credit. It is a step that never was taken before, and has had a prodigious effect to stop the run which was begun.' Later in the year, a great subscription was raised at the Guildhall to buy comforts for the troops, mostly warm clothing for wear in the forthcoming winter campaign. Walpole also noted: 'The merchants are very zealous and are opening a great subscription for raising troops.' In all, £18,435 (over £2 million in modern reckoning) was contributed.[18]

Meanwhile, some Londoners sympathised with the Jacobites. Nicholas Rogers's exhaustive study of sedition within the capital indicates that ninety-seven people were accused of uttering seditious words in 1745–6 (a tiny number considering London's overall population. In fact, proportionately, Jacobitism was stronger in Leeds). Henry and Alice Dainton, a Marylebone excise officer and his wife, were accused of denouncing the King and the bishops as 'the greatest Rogues in England' and hoping that they would 'soon have the Pretender to rectify and redress these grievances'. Isaac Sugden, a Holborn weaver, was accused of saying, 'James the 3rd and his family' were 'the right heirs to the Crown and no others'. Others drank the health of the Jacobite cause – these were mainly Irish Catholics. These Jacobites were disparate individuals, unconnected with one another. This was in no way a mass movement, as Jacobitism had been in London in 1715–1716, when large numbers gathered to support the Jacobite cause. Although Charles Haydon announced that 100,000 Londoners would march out to support the Jacobites in 1745, none did so.[19]

Some have claimed that the Common Council of the City of London – often a thorn in the flesh of the national government – was sympathetic towards Jacobitism. Certainly, in the 1747 General Election, their enemies portrayed them as such. According to Fielding, the councillors 'openly drew their corks in the Pretender's favour' as the Jacobite army marched south. It was also thought, in August 1746, that some Londoners, 'several of them persons of note', had sent money (to the tune of £400,000 or about £50 million in today's money) to aid the rebellion. Yet, according to the Jacobite John Murray, 'there was never any money remitted from England to the Prince since his landing in Scotland'. But, after the rebellion, Murray claimed, 'Dr Barry, a physician in London was employed as an agent: that there were many Persons in the city well affected to the Prince.' Sir James MacDonald claimed: 'We were also told that the City of London in council had decided to send a deputation to meet

H.R.H. on his arrival.' The alleged Jacobites stated that they were innocent (after the rebellion was over) and such charges were merely party political propaganda. One wrote: 'The Phantom of Jacobitism is made to appear in such terrible shapes.' It is hard to know the truth of these accusations and counter-accusations, but no contemporary reports sustain the idea of ardent Jacobitism among the councillors and merchants of the City.[20]

There were a number of rumours and false alarms, most of which were anti-Catholic in tone. Birch claimed there were 150,000 Catholics in London: 'much more formidable than what I could have imagined'. There was a report of a Te Deum being sung at a Catholic chapel in Hampstead shortly after Prestonpans, in thanks for the Jacobite victory. In response to these fears, magistrates had Catholic property searched for arms and several priests were arrested.[21]

Yet, although the morale of some civilians was low, for others the emergency produced a different reaction. According to Walpole, when the London weavers heard of the Jacobite advance, they offered the King 1,000 men, others volunteering for service in the Foot Guards. Newcastle confirmed this: 'a considerable number of his good subjects [...] out of zeal for His Majesty's service and for the preservation of our excellent constitution, are desirous of appearing under arms for the present occasion.' James Henshawe, a Londoner, thought that if the Jacobites reached London, their 'little army might have been eaten up here, where nine men in ten were resolved to expose themselves to all hazards in opposition to him.'[22]

There were numerous associations of civilians who formed themselves into quasi-military units. According to the *True Patriot*:

> another sort of spirit hath prevailed amongst the men, particularly in the City of London, where many persons of good fortune, having provided themselves with uniforms, were on Saturday last enlisted as volunteers in the Guards. And on Sunday the Associated independent companies were reviewed in Hyde Park by General Folliott. The lawyers likewise having exercised themselves in arms, have sub-scribed an Engagement to form themselves into a regiment for the defence of His Majesty.[23]

One method the capital's elite had of displaying their loyalty was by subscribing to the Middlesex Association, an organisation that raised money to encourage regular army recruitment. In Middlesex, £9,616 17s was raised (more than £1 million in modern reckoning). Noblemen paid the most – the Lords Lieutenant of Middlesex subscribed £500. These subscription lists give a basic index of loyalty to the Hanoverian state. Hugh Smithson, a Tory MP, subscribed £300, although the county's other Tory MP, Roger Newdigate, conspicuously did not. Nor did Lords Granville and Bath, both enemies of the government.

Other civilian forces included the London Trained Bands. These were under the command of the City of London and organised into six regiments. They patrolled the streets and gates of the City from dusk to dawn, with orders to stop any suspicious strangers. These were, perhaps, the least inefficient of irregular formations and regiments marched out of London to join the regulars at Finchley. The Tower Hamlets Militia was another quasi-military body summoned into being. And there were others, often financed by voluntary subscriptions of the wealthy. Walpole recalled paying towards the upkeep of one such body. Workmen at the dockyards of Deptford and Woolwich were formed into quasi-military units.

Humbler bodies also declared their aim of raising money and men for the capital's defence. Tower Hamlets raised £3,000 (almost £400,000 in modern terms) and Hackney £1,500. A subscription was begun at Camberwell and Peckham to maintain 200 armed and uniformed men, paying them one shilling each per day (twice the rate of a regular infantryman). A subscription at Rotherhithe promised £1,240. Stoke Newington subscribed £700 and the parishes of Tottenham, Edmonton and Enfield almost as much. At Southwark, it was envisaged that 150 grenadiers would be raised for service against the rebellion and a subscription was opened to encourage men to enlist. Sir Abraham Shard raised, clothed and armed fifty men in Southwark for a period of six months. When Colonel Sowle's soldiers marched through Southwark in early November, 100 men joined, some of whom may have been those raised by Shard and others. There was also an association of Billingsgate porters, volunteer companies in the City and Westminster, regiments of lawyers, weavers and actors. Others enlisted in the regulars – 300 from St Martin's were alleged to have done so – training being provided by the Chelsea pensioners.

Less successful was the Middlesex militia. Orders were given for its formation in mid-December but doubts regarding its efficacy soon became apparent. First, the deputy lieutenants thought that 'as subscriptions of money have been made in all parishes for enlisting men in His Majesty's Land Forces', there would be little enthusiasm for further expenses. And second, once the Jacobites began their retreat, there seemed little reason to spend time and money on a receding danger.[24] Despite their enthusiasm, the efficiency of these various forces is questionable. Militia and volunteer forces had not been effective against the Jacobites so far in the campaign. The weavers who volunteered were not even armed until 10 December, so could scarcely be proficient in the use of these weapons. Nevertheless, these amateur soldiers effectively demonstrated London's loyalism as a potent political force.

During the moment of greatest crisis, 6 December, Newcastle (again, contrary to Johnstone) instructed Henry Marshall, Lord Mayor of London, to be 'very vigilant in preventing, or suppressing any Disorders or Tumults; and so seize any persons that may be assembled together, in a riotous manner'.[25] Marshall seems to have obeyed Newcastle's orders, for on 7 December a number of instructions were noted, issued for security measures to be implemented in the capital. The Trained Bands were to patrol and guard the city squares and avenues. Alarm posts were to be placed at strategic points in the suburbs. Entrances to the city were to be obstructed, a return of horses was to be made and marshals were to ensure constables obeyed their orders. Signals at the Tower were planned to summon the Trained Bands and Guards to any danger point.

Morale was boosted by the fact that George II had refused to quit, declaring that 'he intended to remain and die King of England'. And what was more, George was planning to lead the forces gathering on Finchley Common in person. The King was well known for his physical bravery – only two years before he had led his troops to victory over the French at Dettingen. Likewise, Newcastle was not about to throw in his lot with the Jacobites. He was busy preparing the defence of the capital against insurgents within, as well as any invading armies without.[26]

There were other signs that those in the metropolis were loyal to the status quo. An effigy of the Pope was burnt at Deptford on 5 November, watched by a large crowd, singing 'God Save the King'. The King's birthday on 11 October was celebrated, with bonfires and beer. House windows were lit up. At the Royal Exchange, the Pretender's (Bonnie Prince Charlie's) declaration was burnt 'amidst the repeated Acclamations of a prodigious number of People'. Apparently, 'the Populace carried the Effigy of the Pretender, hanging on a Gibbet, thro' the City, attended by six Butchers with their Mock Musick'. On a more sedate note, Miss Gertrude Saville noted in her diary: 'The King's Birthday observed in a most uncommon loyal manner; almost every House illuminated – mine among the rest.'[27]

The capital's clergy preached against the Jacobites. Thomas Anguish, Rector of St Nicholas's Deptford, claimed Popery would 'drench our streets in blood'. The rebels and their supporters were attacked. James Bate of St Paul's Deptford, stated: 'the Nation is invaded by a desperate Band of hungry popish vagabonds and Cut-throats [...] by the help of France and Spain'. He added that horrors were in the offing because of the 'craving demands of the Pope and the French [...] the gaping mouths of his hungry and naked Fiends of the north' – the Scots. Likewise, Thomas Wingfield, lecturer at St Thomas's, Southwark, told his listeners that this was not a case of 'Preaching up of Politicks and Party Matters', adding that George II stood for liberty and civil and religious rights against the prospect of Popery.[28]

The churches rang their bells on Loyalist occasions, such the anniversary of the King's birthday on 11 October, that of his coronation on 30 October, and 5 November – a red-letter day for Protestants on account of their twofold delivery from popery: the foiling of a Catholic plot to blow up Parliament in 1605 and the arrival in England of William of Orange in 1688. St Mary's, Acton, St Mary's, Harrow, and St George's, Hanworth, all rang their bells on these three occasions. In the following year, bells rang again to mark victory over the Jacobites. St John the Baptist's, Pinner, rang bells on 14 May, presumably to celebrate Cumberland's victory at Culloden four weeks earlier. Curiously enough, the ringers at St Mary's, Norwood, received a leg of pork for ringing on 5 November. The bells of St Nicholas's Deptford rang on every conceivable occasion – apart from those mentioned above, they rang for Cumberland's birthday and on 'receiving the joyful News of the Duke of Cumberland's overcoming the Rebels'.[29]

As matters transpired, the leaders of the Jacobite army decided to retreat, marching northwards on 6 December. In part this was because of the uncertain reception they feared they would receive in London, even if they defeated George's regular armies in the field. Lord George Murray, a Jacobite general, argued thus:

> suppose the army was to slip the King's and the Duke's army and get into London, the success of the affair would entirely depend upon the mobs declaring for or against it, and that if the mob had been much inclined to his cause, since his march into England, that to be sure some of his friends in London would have fallen upon some method to have let him know it. But if the mob was against the affair 4,500 men would not make a great figure in London.[30]

So much for mass Jacobite support in London.

Why did Londoners act in the way they did; viz. in a manner to support the status quo? The Hanoverian monarchs may not have been popular, but they were preferable to the alternative. The Stuarts were Catholic and anti-Catholicism was a virulent force in eighteenth-century England, as seen by the rioting against Catholic chapels in 1688 and 1780. Also, the Jacobites were allied to France, which was equated with tyranny as well as Catholicism. Finally, Loyalist propaganda tapped the libertarian vein running through London politics.

This was the last time an army tried to march on London. The Jacobite army was crushed at Culloden in 1746 and Londoners celebrated the victory. There were other Jacobite conspiracies in the 1750s but they came to nothing. Never again would a Jacobite army materialise on British soil. Meanwhile, anti-Catholicism remained a strong force among Londoners – and elsewhere – and could be used by unscrupulous figures for their own ends.

The Gordon Riots 1780

Jacobitism was virtually dead, to be replaced by political Radicalism as a major force in London street politics in the 1760s. The leading agent was John Wilkes, a journalist and MP, who earned the wrath of the government and the popularity of the crowd. There were riots in London on his behalf and on one occasion, several men were killed by troops. Although, by the following decade, Wilkes had settled down as a respectable politician, the Radical cause remained strong. Groups throughout Britain demanded political reform. With the rise of literacy, men denied a political voice – artisans, craftsmen and small merchants – demanded their say, which, unsurprisingly, threatened the status quo. And yet, on the whole, these men were not revolutionaries: nevertheless, the government viewed them as such. The situation was exacerbated by the American Revolutionary War of 1775–1781, opposed by many in Britain, who viewed the government as tyrannical and incompetent, both at home and abroad.

Yet in 1780, London was terrorised not by Radicals but by a more 'traditional' enemy. According to *The Gentleman's Magazine*, in 1780, 'no event has happened that will be read by future generations with so much surprise and astonishment as what we are now about to relate'. The Gordon Riots were the worst riots that ever occurred in England. They lasted longer than other riots, more people were killed (only one death was recorded in 1715 and none in 1688) and there was more damage to property. The root cause was continuing anti-Catholicism, so prevalent among the majority of England's population. Yet the views of the political elite were shifting towards religious toleration. In 1778 the Catholic Relief Bill became law. This made Catholic schools legal, ended the prosecution of priests and made it lawful for Catholics to convey (that is, sell) property as they pleased. That many of these practices were already permissible was not the point – the new law made them explicit.[31]

Lord George Gordon, a young Scottish peer, was outraged by the Catholic Relief Bill and soon found others who agreed with him. During 1779 a number of Protestant societies were established throughout Britain with the aim of putting pressure on MPs and peers to repeal the Act. Such lobbying was legal, but some of Gordon's supporters attacked Catholics and their property in Scotland, and this was something entirely different.

It was in the summer of 1780 that Gordon's campaign took an ugly turn in England. At first all seemed well. He summoned his supporters to lobby Parliament and they answered his call, assembling in vast numbers to present a huge petition, demanding the repeal of the Act. What happened next would remain forever in the memory of all Londoners living in the capital at that time. As that effete man of letters, Horace Walpole, wrote:

> I remember the Excise, and the Gin Act, [both of which provoked rioting in London] and the rebels at Derby, and the Wilkes' interlude, and the French at Plymouth – or I should have a very bad memory – but I never till last night saw London and Southwark in flames.[32]

Dr Samuel Johnson (1709–1784) was also affected, writing to Mrs Theale:

> One might see the glare of conflagration fill the sky from many parts. The sight was dreadful. Such a time of terror. You have been happy in not seeing.[33]

On Friday, 2 June, several thousand of Gordon's supporters gathered at St George's Fields and at noon they marched on Parliament, where they surrounded all its entrances. One contemporary estimate put their number at 100,000, though this is probably an exaggeration. Some shouted 'No Popery!' Lords and MPs were harangued as they tried to enter the House. Some, such as Lord Bathurst and the Bishop of Lichfield were assaulted, others were forced to swear that they would vote to repeal the Act. Gordon harangued the mob, urging them on. When the petition for repeal was presented to the House, it was overwhelmingly rejected, but the mob dispersed when threatened with troops. The dangers of the day, however, were far from over. The mob merely moved elsewhere, attacking Catholic chapels in Duke Street and Warwick Street, 'both of which they in a great measure demolished'. Eventually, troops dispersed the rioters, several of whom were arrested.[34]

The following day was peaceful, so 'sober people were rejoicing that the zealots for religion had exhausted their rage, and that peace and good order were again restored'. Such hopes were disappointed when fresh troubles broke out on Sunday. Houses and chapels belonging to Catholics in Moorfields were attacked and stripped of furniture. Chapels had their altars, pulpits, pews and all their ornamentation ripped out and burnt in the streets. On Monday, 5 June, the devastation continued. More Catholic property was destroyed, as well as houses belonging to men who had borne witness against those taken on Friday. Sir George Saville, MP, who had been prominent in promoting the Catholic Relief Act, also had his house broken into and the internal fittings were burnt.

The forces of authority did little except to offer a reward of £500 (over £40,000 in modern reckoning) to anyone who could identify the culprits who had destroyed two chapels belonging to foreign embassies.[35]

There was a greater show of military force on 6 June, when troops were stationed at the Tower of London, the Houses of Parliament and other open spaces within the capital. Their presence did not initially deter the mob, which split into smaller groups that evening. Newgate Prison was attacked and the prisoners – numbering about 300, including convicted killers – were released and the place burnt to the ground. Properties belonging to Catholics, magistrates and lawyers who had acted against the rioters, were broken into and the furnishings burnt. Those whose houses were attacked could do nothing but flee with only the clothes they stood up in. It was only after Lord Mansfield's possessions had gone up in smoke that a party of soldiers arrived. The Riot Act was read by a magistrate, but the mob refused to disperse. Then the order was given to open fire. Several men and women in the mob were wounded, but this did not stop the remaining rioters from completing their work of destruction.

The rioting was at its height on Wednesday 7 June. Although, according to *The Annual Register*, 'It is impossible to give any adequate description of the events of Wednesday', an attempt must be made. More Catholic property was attacked. Prominent among these was the great distillery of Mr Langdale in Holborn. Damage estimated at £100,000 (approximately £10 million in today's money) was caused. Other businessmen took precautionary measures to avoid the wrath of the rioters. Shopkeepers shut up shop and tried to protect their premises by pretending to sympathise with the mob. This they did by chalking 'No Popery' on the walls and by hanging out flags of blue silk – the colour adopted by the mob. Likewise, Jewish shopkeepers in Houndsditch chalked, 'This house a True Protestant' on their property. Where people fled their homes, they wrote on the walls, 'Empty, but no Popery'. According to Fanny Burney, 'All the stage coaches that came into Bath from London are chalked on with "No Popery".' But no one felt secure. Some fled or had their possessions removed, Johnson writing that 'Mr Strachan moved what he could, and advised me to take care of myself'.[36]

Some civilians reacted militantly. Lawyers and law students from the Inns of Court armed themselves in order to defend their property if the need arose. They were left unmolested. As William Pitt (1759–1806) wrote:

> Several very respectable lawyers have appeared with muskets on their shoulders, to the no small diversion of all spectators. Unluckily the Appearance of Danger ended just as we embodied, and our military Ardour has been thrown away.[37]

But some behaved in a reckless manner. At the height of the rioting, according to Charlotte Burney, many people still attended the pleasure gardens at Ranelagh, though they knew their homes might be burnt by the rioters.

By evening, parts of London were on fire. Prisons – such as the King's Bench, Fleet and the New Bridewell – were burnt, as were other domestic properties. Throughout London, there were thirty-six separate blazes. Attempts to extinguish them were hindered, because fire engines were cut to pieces by the rioters. The wealthy had already fled London in their coaches. Others had more difficulty. According to Walpole, there were 'Women and children screaming, running out of doors, with what they could save, and knocking one another down with their loads in confusion.' The noise of the flames and the 'dreadful reports of soldiers muskets' were heard. Anarchy had been let loose. There were also attempts to break into the Bank of England, but they were beaten off, once the rioters began suffering casualties. According to Johnson:

> It is agreed that if they had seized the Bank on Tuesday, at the height of the panic, when no resistance had been prepared, they might have carried irrevocably away whatever they had found; but the rioters attempted the Bank on Wednesday night, but in great number; and like other thieves, with a great resolution. Jack Wilkes headed the party that drove them away. Jack, who was always for order and decency, declares that if he be trusted with power, he will not leave a rioter alive.[38]

Ironically, it took the Gordon riots to bring the King and Wilkes – once deadly enemies – together.

It was on the Thursday, 8 June, that the army and the militia regained control of the streets, which now resembled a battlefield. There were no further demonstrations on this day, as rioters were arrested. Lord Gordon was also taken prisoner. Likewise, Friday was peaceful, but there remained a sense of unease. This was due, in part, to the fact that London was under martial law. The army had powers to shoot rioters on sight – no need for a magistrate to read the Riot Act beforehand. The troops were assisted by armed associations of Londoners – groups of men who armed themselves against the rioters, and who proved themselves just as lethal.

The most common reaction after the riots was one of relief.

But the people who suffered most bodily harm – as opposed to being terrorised – were the rioters themselves. Some of alcohol poisoning, after drinking unadulterated spirits by the pail, stolen from Langdale's brewery.

Others died in the flames and damage inflicted by collapsing buildings. A further 210 were killed by troops and seventy-five others later died of wounds. Finally, some thirty-five were executed.

The rioters were made up of many different kinds of people. Some were lads in their early teens, others mature women. One man was an apothecary, another an ex-soldier, yet another a hangman. But the phenomenon was not totally anarchic: ringleaders had orchestrated much of the destruction wrought by the mob.

The riots lasted so long, and were so destructive, because magistrates failed to act as they should have done. George III referred at this time to 'the supineness of the magistrates'. This was partly because the laws pertaining to riots were somewhat ambiguous. Those responsible for shooting rioters dead – whether magistrates or soldiers – could be, and had been, put on trial for murder. Such had happened as recently as 1768, and although those accused were acquitted, the lesson was not lost on London's magistrates. Furthermore, the magistrates had been intimidated by the sheer scale of destruction, especially the demolition of houses belonging to prominent magistrates like John Fielding and Justice Hyde.[39]

George III, however, was made of sterner stuff. He wrote that: 'I fear without more vigour this will not subside; indeed unless exemplary punishments is procured, it will remain a lasting disgrace, and will be a precedent for future commotion.' Sir Horace Mann, a diplomat, later agreed, writing: 'I am not cruel, but I own to you that I wish that the troops had fired on the mob the instant the civil magistrates authorised them to do it.' Johnson approved of stern measures, and wrote that the King had 'saved the town from calamities' and rejoiced that 'Government now acts again with its proper force'.[40]

Few sympathised with the rioters, including many anti-Catholics. Walpole told one of his correspondents: 'I always, as you know well, disliked and condemned the repeal of the Popish statutes, and am steadfast in that opinion, but I abhor such Protestantism as breathes the soul of Popery, and commences a reform by attempting a massacre.' Likewise, Johnson sympathised with the Catholics, recording that 'several inoffensive papists have been plundered'.[41]

After the rioting, people once more took to the streets. Charlotte Burney told her sister in Bath that 'the streets were never more crowded – everybody is wandering about in order to see the ruins of the places that the mob have destroyed'. Yet there was still danger for the unwary and some took advantage of the disorder. As Charlotte explained:

> There have been gangs of women going about to rob and plunder.
> Miss Kirwans went out on Friday afternoon to walk in the Museum

gardens, and was stopped by a set of women and robbed of all the money they had.[42]

Conspiracy theories abounded as to the cause of the disturbances. Many thought that anti-Catholicism was but a smokescreen. With the country at war with France, Spain and the rebellious American colonies, some believed that foreign agents might be responsible. Some thought it had been planned by criminals in order to burn and destroy. Others, including Walpole, believed that it was a government plot aimed at strengthening a weakened state. It was believed by some that the government might use the rioting as a pretext to introduce military rule, or at least install a permanent police force to overawe their opponents. But, as with most conspiracy theories, no evidence ever came to light. Anti-Catholicism was probably the main motivation for most of the rioters, at least at first. Dr Johnson remarked: 'Whatever some may maintain, I am satisfied that there was no combination or plan, either domestic or foreign.'[43]

It is ironic that a Frenchman in London at the time of the rioting observed that such would never happen in Paris: in the following decade the French King was executed by revolutionaries and many thousands massacred during Robespierre's reign of terror. One positive effect of the Gordon Riots was that it caused a reaction against such disorders and a desire that such should never happen again. During the violent upheavals in France in the following years, there was no such violence in London.

Finally, the Gordon riots did not help the Radical cause, and indeed made many of its followers more cautious. Many moderate reformers were frightened by the bloodshed and chaos they had seen or heard about and opted for a quiet life. Meanwhile, the conservatives' fear of the mob was vindicated. Certainly the government was strengthened by the quelling of the riots and its prestige temporarily rose. Yet a permanent civilian police force was not introduced till almost half a century later. This was also the last major religious riot in London, but religion was to resurface as a reason for violence in a later century.

The Clerkenwell Riot 1833

Despite – or perhaps because of – the French Revolutionary and Napoleonic Wars of 1793–1815, London was fairly quiet. Yet political storm clouds were simmering. Calls for Parliamentary reform had existed since the 1780s and, with the coming of a Whig government in 1830, which promised such, expectations were high. Very few adult men could vote in 1830 and many thought the right to vote should be extended – by force if necessary. As Parliament debated the issue, there was trouble on the streets of London in 1831, but the Reform Act was passed in the following year, abolishing rotten boroughs (Parliamentary constituencies where only a few voters elected the MPs) and extending the franchise. Unlike previous riots, there was no religious dimension.

But many thought the Act too limited, that it did not go far enough in its provisions (only a minority of adult males were eligible to vote, as voting rights were dependent on ownership of property). Despite increasing male suffrage, voters – the upper and middle classes – were still in the minority (and women had no right to vote at all). Associations – largely composed of working men – sprang up to pressurise the government into granting them the vote. The authorities viewed these demands as dangerous and would not concede. The latter could now deploy a new force to protect the status quo – the Metropolitan Police, formed in 1829, and capable of controlling violent protest. This controversial new force was unpopular, many viewing it as a paramilitary instrument of repression. Hostility to the police was therefore widespread. A fatal clash between the forces of political Radicalism and those of law and order occurred on 13 May 1833.

The committee of the National Union of the Working Classes was one key Radical group. It announced a meeting on the morning of Monday, 13 May, to be held at Calthorpe Street, Cold Bath Fields. This was to discuss the holding of a National Convention 'as the only means of obtaining and securing the rights of the people'. The government, however, announced that such a meeting was illegal and threatened strong action: none should attend the meeting unless they wished to be arrested.[44]

But government warnings did not deter the Radicals. People began congregating from eleven in the morning on 13 May. By two o'clock, between 3,000–4,000 were present. But not all were supporters of peaceful reform: some had been drinking heavily prior to the meeting, and some were armed with loaded sticks (wooden sticks reinforced with metal), knives and concealed daggers. The committee, consisting of six men, was at the Union public house on Bagnigge-Wells, discussing who should address the crowd first. It was decided that young James Lee should do so and, at about three, he clambered onto a caravan hired for the purpose. Others joined him, but the owner of the caravan did not like the way matters were progressing and drove off, obliging the Radicals to jump off. The authorities had also assembled forces in the vicinity. In the afternoon, the police marched into the locality, taking up quarters at the riding school of the London Volunteers and other stables nearby. One contemporary source put their number at 1,700. The police commissioners, Colonel Rowan and Richard Mayne, were also in attendance. Several officers of the Lifeguards were in civilian clothes nearby, and had a detachment of troopers on hand, in case they were needed.

Lee was carried on the shoulders of the crowd and he proposed that a confederate, Mr Mee, should address them first. He did so, and urged them to 'beware of those hirelings of the Government, who were paid to induce them to commit a breach of the peace'. It was then that an additional 150 men arrived carrying banners, on which was written 'Liberty or Death', with a skull and crossbones on a black ground with a red border. Another bore the slogan 'Holy Alliance of the Working Classes', another 'Equal Rights and Equal Justice'. There was also the tricolour flag of Revolutionary and Napoleonic France and the Republican flag of America. One man carried a pole with a revolutionary cap on it. The crowd made deafening cheers when they arrived.[45]

They were not the only new arrivals on the scene. Several detachments of police marched with military precision into the street. This raised the tension immediately. People among the crowd were apprehensive but when the man bearing the 'Liberty or Death' flag shouted, 'Men be firm!' their spirits rallied. Some cried out 'Down with them, Liberty or Death!' and appeared to be ready for anything. Another shout to their speakers was: 'Go on, go on!' The police columns then halted in the middle of the street.[46]

What happened next depends on which account a reader chooses to believe. The account in *The Gentleman's Magazine* stated 'the police [...] commenced a general and indiscriminate attack on the populace'. However, *The Annual Register* put it differently. It stated the police had orders to remain calm as they walked forward, truncheons in hand, to arrest the speaker. It was then that they 'were instantly attacked by the mob'. What is clear is that the Riot Act was not read and there was no attempt to disperse the mob before the police moved in.[47]

In the hand-to-hand fight that followed, both sides sustained some casualties. One source claims that some women were attacked. According to a source sympathetic to the crowd, even those men who tried to run away or to parley, were assaulted. A Radical source claimed that local inhabitants cried 'Shame! Shame!' and 'Mercy! Mercy!' Policemen also sustained wounds when they tried to seize the offending banners. Sergeant Harrison was struck on the arm, but the worst was to come. Constable Robert Culley was stabbed in the body by a stiletto and soon died. An eyewitness, Mary Hamilton, later described his murder as being unprovoked. One source claims the mob made a further attack on the police in order to regain the banners they had lost, but it was repelled. Elsewhere in the locality, a crowd attacked another detachment of police, throwing stones at them. Eventually, the crowd was dispersed and a number of arrests were made. By four o'clock it was all over.

When an inquest was held on the body of Culley, the jury wished to justify his killing on the grounds that the meeting was legal or that, if not, it was not legally dispersed by a magistrate reading the Riot Act. After several days, the jury decided that the verdict should be justifiable homicide on the grounds that police conduct had been 'ferocious, brutal and unprovoked'. Although the coroner thought their judgement perverse and tried to argue an alternative verdict with them, they persisted in their opinion and were cheered by many in the courtroom for their pains. When Culley was buried, his funeral was the scene of protests by crowds hostile to the police. Even among the government, some were unsympathetic towards the police, Lord Holland noting: 'the police [. . .] acted with precipitation and violence in the late affray at Cold Bath Fields and were in the wrong'.[48]

It needs to be stated that the early police were widely unpopular throughout society. Some saw them as agents of an oppressive government. Some objected to their cost. Few welcomed their presence on the streets of London.

The government's lawyers decided to change the verdict to one of wilful murder. One George Fursey was charged with the crime, because he had stabbed two other constables on the same occasion. These two officers said that Fursey was indeed the man who had stabbed them, and he was committed for trial at the Old Bailey. Yet Fursey was eventually acquitted. A Select Committee set up to investigate the matter exonerated the police of any blame, claiming that only seventy policemen had been involved in the affray and that there were avenues of escape open to any of the crowd who wished to flee. Those on the side of the crowd, however, claimed this was a mere whitewash. At the end of the day, the meeting had not achieved anything and further reforms had to wait decades. The principal loser was Mrs Culley, a young widow who was expecting her first child. Although Radical groups continued, the franchise was not extended until 1867 and even then, universal male suffrage was not accomplished. The demonstrators in 1833 achieved nothing positive.

Fenianism 1867
Rioting was not the only form of violent outburst in the nineteenth century, for terrorism first raised its head at this time.

In this instance, its origins lay in Ireland. The country had been ruled by Britain for centuries, but many were unhappy with the status quo. Many Irishmen extolled peaceful means for achieving Home Rule. Several English politicians sympathised – up to a point – including William Gladstone, a towering figure in Victorian politics. But some Irish nationalists sought a swifter – more violent – solution. These were known as the Fenians. Founded in Ireland in 1858 by James Stephens, the organisation took its name from 'Fianna' – legendary Irish warriors. The activities of the Fenians soon spread to English cities like Chester, Liverpool and London – and even as far afield as America.

The worst single attack occurred in December 1867. Richard Burke, a leading Fenian, was incarcerated in Clerkenwell House of Detention, awaiting trial. A plot was hatched to rescue him by blowing a hole in the prison wall. Despite letters warning Sir Richard Mayne, the Police Commissioner, no precautions were taken. The explosion, which took place on the evening of 13 December, demolished most of the houses in nearby Corporation Lane. Twelve people died and at least forty were injured. Some 200 houses were damaged and 600 families were affected. Material damage was estimated at £12,000 (almost £800,000 in modern terms). To make matters worse, there had also been some looting, and a woman recalled, 'I miss many things, which I suppose were carried off by some of the persons who entered in the confusion.' And yet, despite the spectacular nature of the event, the Fenians failed to rescue Burke.[49]

A certain Mr Herring was quick to make a public appeal for money on behalf of those who had suffered. This raised the ire of the Reverend Robert Maguire, vicar of Clerkenwell. He wrote that Herring:

> plainly exceeded the bounds of both duty and necessity [...] All the locality affected by the explosion is in my parish [...] It is far from Mr Herring's district, and he is in no respect called upon to act while the parochial staff are actively engaged in the matter.

Herring later apologised to Maguire, claiming he acted 'on the spur of the moment' and Maguire wrote to say 'I can quite understand this'. Afterwards, the two worked together to help the needy.[50] In fact, Maguire had been active from the onset of the tragedy. As he wrote:

> I hastened down immediately to the scene of the explosion and then to the hospitals, where I spent the whole of the evening and until past midnight.

Herring also helped by visiting all the streets affected by the blast in order to see what needs had to be met and helped to distribute fifty blankets given by the East London Relief Association.[51]

Those injured in the blasts were sent to hospitals, apparently receiving satisfactory treatment. Dr Jenner reported thus to Queen Victoria, who was most concerned about their predicament: 'The patients in both hospitals assured me that they want for nothing, and that everyone is most kind and attentive.'[52]

Government intervention in what would be called a 'humanitarian crisis' in the later twentieth century, was unheard-of in the nineteenth. Private assistance was the norm. There was a meeting on 16 December and a committee was formed, chaired by Maguire. Herring also sat on the committee. Maguire promised that 'There shall be no lack of active interest in the care of the sufferers and their families.' Many people came forward with donations of money, which the committee used to provide temporary relief by buying blankets and clothing, and in paying for temporary accommodation. Maguire wrote: 'The liberality of the public is most gracious in this distressing matter.' In order to advertise this fund, statements listing donors and their sums were published in the press. By 7 January 1868 £6,691 1s 9d had been raised by this method (approximately £440,000 in modern money). Parcels of clothing were also received.[53]

Yet the committee did not think that this money would be sufficient to meet all their needs. It was estimated that between £12,000–15,000 would be required to repair all damage. As Maguire said, 'Private benevolence had its limits.' He and others were given an audience at Downing Street to discuss the matter with the government. The Chancellor was polite but left them in no doubt that the government would not release any public funds, for this was a matter for private efforts alone (as with the Irish Potato Famine of the 1840s).[54]

There was another side to the coin, too. A potential backlash against the large numbers of Irish in London was feared, especially if there was another bombing on the same scale. Sir Digby Seymour, an Irish lawyer in London, wrote to *The Times* to allay these suspicions, writing:

> Sir, I believe the vast majority of my countrymen in London are at heart loyal and as true as any man in Her majesty's dominions. I believe that the miscreants who planned the desperate outrage of Clerkenwell, if Irishmen by name or birth, are the miserable and misguided tools of fancy and corruption.

Yet he had, as yet, no evidence to back his words.[55] Seymour later referred to steps that had been taken against his fellow countrymen in London:

> when the news of that terrible atrocity had been circulated through-out the country it became apparent that the employers of Irish labour in this country began to distrust their employees, and to doubt especially whether they could continue the joint employment of English and Irish labour. In some instances Irishmen had actually been discharged from their employment.[56]

Therefore, in an attempt to prevent such unfair suspicions, in January 1868, Seymour took it upon himself to gather a petition of signatures of Irishmen in London, stating their abhorrence of the Clerkenwell atrocity and their loyalty to the Queen. Seymour hoped it would be a 'proud and glorious muster-roll of Irish Loyalists resident in the metropolis of the empire'. Some 22,603 were willing to sign Seymour's petition, and those that did 'represented every branch of profession, merchandise, trade and opinion in the city of London'. Employers were given copies of the petition for their Irish employees to sign, but Seymour stressed that no pressure should be put on anyone to comply. In fact, many signed it freely without any prompting. And although Irish clergy signed the petition, they refrained from instructing their parishioners to do so, for again, this was seen as using undue influence. One clergyman of an East London parish had convinced the few of his parishioners with Fenian sympathies to drop them. The petition appears to have been a great success in demonstrating that the majority of Irishmen in London were as opposed to terrorism as anyone else.[57]

The perpetrator of the Fenian outrage, one Michael Barrett, was tried and executed, being the last man in England to be hanged in public. A large and peaceful crowd watched him die. In the same year, the Fenian movement, riven by internal dissension and attacked by the Roman Catholic Church, dissolved.

There were other Fenian dynamite outrages in the years 1883–1885 with tube and railway stations being attacked, as well as attempts to blow up the House of Commons, London Bridge and Nelson's Column. Most of these caused little damage and no one was killed.

For instance, on the evening of 2 January 1885, there was a bomb attack on an Underground train travelling from King's Cross to Gower Street. Although the carriage lights went out and women screamed, only four people received minor injuries. The passengers were evacuated. However, 'in the street above, great alarm was caused by the violence of the shock'. An eyewitness wrote to *The Times* newspaper to report his disgust at the 'cowardly' criminals and the slackness of the government.[58]

After 1885, the bombings came to an end. Fenianism as a direct form of action failed, but the Irish nationalist cause did not. The 'Irish Question' – as it was called by English politicians – thus remained. A number of reforms were introduced, giving Irishmen greater freedoms. At the eve of the twentieth century, the Liberal government was proposing Home Rule for a united Ireland. The First World War intervened, but following that – and a brief but bitter war – Ireland was partitioned between the largely Catholic South and the mostly Protestant North in 1921.

The Trafalgar Square Riot 1887
Radical politics were the politics of Socialism in the late nineteenth century. Despite the fact that London was the capital of a worldwide empire, it was, as

ever, divided between the haves and the have-nots. Incidents such as the one about to be described made the social divisions all the more glaring. For late Victorian Radicals and socialists, Bloody Sunday referred to the events of 13 November 1887. Polite society, however, had a different version.

The politics of the late nineteenth century differed from that of the 1830s. There had been two further Reform Acts, in 1867 and 1885, which had further extended the franchise among the adult male population, though this was still short of universal male suffrage. Furthermore, trades unions were now legitimate associations and, as noted, there was agitation in Ireland for political reform. In November 1887 tensions ran even higher due to violent clashes between police and demonstrators in Chicago, where two anarchists were later hanged. The Metropolitan Radical Association, in order to further its aim of demanding 'the release of Mr William O'Brien and other Irish patriots' – Irishmen imprisoned in London – decided to call a mass meeting in Central London. They sent circulars all over the capital in order to attract the maximum number of people. Backed by the Cabinet, Sir Charles Warren, Commissioner of the Metropolitan Police, had already issued an order forbidding public meetings in Trafalgar Square, although this was aimed at preventing gatherings of the unemployed. And yet, it was only legal to disperse meetings if they became disorderly.[59] Warren's ban on meetings backfired. It had the effect of encouraging other groups – such as the Social Democratic Federation and the Socialist League – to close ranks with the Metropolitan Radical Association, insisting on the right to hold meetings at Trafalgar Square 'at all hazards'. These organisations called forth the men of South and East London to attend, asserting that:

> the right of public meeting is denied by the usage of a military and despotic filibuster. Are you prepared to submit? If not, come in tens of thousands. Preserve your dear bought liberties.[60]

And so the Radicals were resolved to meet at the square. On 11 November, however, when a deputation met the Home Secretary, the latter replied that Trafalgar Square was a possession of the Crown and could only be used by the public at the pleasure of the former, and this had been enshrined in law in 1844. But this pronouncement had no effect on the Radicals, who met the following day to discuss matters. Mrs Annie Besant said she would attend and, by their sheer weight of numbers, they would surely prevail. Mr Aveling advocated a hard-line approach. He said they should go to Trafalgar Square 'with the deliberate intention of showing physical force if necessary'. In order to keep the police guessing, the Radicals had not informed them of the time of the meeting, as was usual on these occasions.[61]

Meanwhile, Warren had been busy too. His plan was to have a small body of police in Trafalgar Square in the early morning, which was accomplished. Furthermore, there were about 2,000 policemen covering the approaches to the square, formed in ranks two deep – except at the entrance to Whitehall, where they were four deep. Constables also patrolled adjacent roads such as Northumberland Avenue, the Strand and Whitehall. There was a body of 300 policemen around Nelson's Column and 100 mounted officers in reserve. There was even a battalion of Grenadier Guards at Wellington Barracks, plus a regiment of Lifeguards at Horse Guards, should they prove necessary. The forces of law and order appeared formidable indeed.

The demonstrators met in different parts of London before converging on Trafalgar Square. One group met at Clerkenwell. They included Radicals, socialists and Irish Nationalists. Their leaders addressed them before the final march took place.

It was three o'clock when the crowds began their march on Trafalgar Square. Some carried banners proclaiming 'Put your trust in God and keep your powder dry' and 'Disobedience to Tyrants is a duty to God'. Others carried the red flags of Communism. It was at the corner of Ducannon Street and St Martin's Lane that the first confrontation of the day took place, as members of the crowd began hissing at the police. Then, two or three constables were molested, unleashing a charge by mounted police aimed at breaking up the throng. Some demonstrators retaliated by attacking policemen with sticks and several riders were knocked from their horses. Luckily for them, some members of the crowd were sympathetic and helped them remount.[62]

By half-past three the approaches to Trafalgar Square were jam-packed with demonstrators. Several Radicals tried to make speeches but were arrested, the police frequently receiving a battering for their trouble. But Warren's officers continued to assail the crowd, as noted by one observer:

> The police, mounted and on foot, charged in amongst the people, striking indiscriminately in all directions [...] The blood, in most instances, was flowing freely [...] and the spectacle was indeed a sickening one.[63]

By four o'clock the crowds had swelled even further. Their numbers were estimated at about 20,000, but many were spectators. There had been some fighting at the top of Parliament Square but the crowds had been repulsed. Then there was a procession, which included a marching band, led by banner-carrying men marching along Pall Mall. A superintendent on horseback ordered them to return but he was ignored and on they marched. On this, Major Gilbert of the police ordered his men to charge the procession. The police used truncheons and men in the crowd fought back with sticks. The procession broke up and fled, leaving banners on the ground. Elsewhere, there was fighting on the Haymarket, where another procession was barred.

So far, the police had managed to stop the crowds entering Trafalgar Square. It was now that the encounter reached its climax. About 200 men – allegedly headed by two Radical MPs, John Burns and Cunningham Grahame – rushed at the police from the corner of the Strand. It was a very determined onslaught and the police initially lost ground to the chargers. Other constables came to their aid and the attackers were forced to flee.

As the day began to darken, there were still large numbers of people around the square, though not in it. At 4.30pm, two squadrons of Lifeguards rode up from Whitehall with a magistrate at their head. They rode all around the square, between crowds and police, eliciting cheers from both police and onlookers as they went. Soldiers of the Foot Guards also appeared. It was clear to all that the day's action was over, as the authorities had brought over-whelming force to bear. The crowds, who contained sightseers as well as Radicals, began to disperse and by 5.30pm, it was all over. By seven, the last of the soldiers returned to their barracks.

It was now time to survey the scene. Fifty men had been arrested, including Grahame and Burns. At least seventy-five men had been injured and were treated at Charing Cross Hospital. Most had sustained scalp wounds, though one man had been injured by a soldier's bayonet. Some policemen had also been wounded – some knifed, others injured by blunt instruments. A few of their horses had been stabbed.

Letters to *The Times* on following days were supportive of the police. A Chicago policeman, who had witnessed the confrontation, declared 'that the much-abused London police showed a spirit of moderation towards the mob which they would not receive in any American city'. Major General Bray wrote: 'the police officer in command [...] acted admirably and with great decision and judgement'. According to *The Times*:

> There were general rejoicings all over London, especially in the West End, that the police had so effectually succeeded in breaking up the organised disorder on Sunday.[64]

Local middle-class opinion agreed, as the editorial of *The Paddington Times* commented:

> London is to be congratulated upon the decision with which Sir Charles Warren acting under the authority of the Home Secretary, adopted measures last week to put an end to the disorderly and

riotous gatherings which for some week past have made Trafalgar
Square a nuisance and a peril to the inhabitants of the locality.[65]

They had little sympathy for the protestors, termed 'The rough and rowdies
of London [...] whose only object is direct or indirect plunder [...] this
large crowd revels in riot and glories in sedition'. The police behaved with
'commendable forbearance under extreme provocation [...] in self-defence'.
The editorial spoke up in favour of the shopkeepers, allegedly terrorised by the
crowd, and dismissed the leaders of the mob as 'tub-thumping and pot house
politicians', who 'got the broken heads they deserved'. The *Bayswater Chronicle*
agreed, claiming the police were 'as forbearing under the circumstances as
human beings could be'.[66]

But not all agreed with such assessments. Radical clubs in South-East
London met at Rotherhithe and denounced 'the murderous actions of the
police'. They called on their fellows to 'protest loudly against the unwarrantable
police butchery directed by Sir Charles Warren'. A thousand men attended
the meeting. Mr Glanville, a Liberal MP for the constituency who attended the
meeting, said the crowd were unarmed and were 'attacked without the least
provocation'. Another speaker claimed that the whole day had been a conspiracy
by the police to entice people to be bludgeoned by them. It was at this meeting
that the term 'Bloody Sunday' was first coined.[67]

A total of seventy-five complaints were lodged against the police for brutality.
Mr W.T. Stead wrote that the latter's actions had been 'characterised by a
brutality which I have never seen in the whole of my life'. Edward Carpenter,
a socialist, claimed the police deliberately provoked a good-humoured crowd in
order to provoke a riot. The Bermondsey Liberal Club spoke of a 'cowardly
and murderous action by the police in unjustifiably assaulting [...] peaceful and
law-abiding citizens'.[68]

Many middle-class people had seen the large demonstration as a threat
to public order and to their own prosperity. Although there had been little
damage to property, there was a marked loss of trade to those businesses in or
near Trafalgar Square. Many shopkeepers reacted by ingratiating themselves
with the police, sending food hampers to police stations. Some joined the
Special Constabulary. Some among the middle class did not even notice the
riot. Florence Essery, a young lady resident in Westminster at the time, noted
in her diary on the day of the riot: 'I did not go out until the evening and then
went to St Margaret's and heard the new curate, Mr Savage.'[69]

None of the police faced any legal action after the riot. The two Radical
MPs, Burns and Grahame, endured short prison sentences. Other men were
fined or gaoled.

But it was only some weeks later that the full cost was known. Alfred Linell, a young Radical who had taken part in the demonstration, was one of the injured. On 3 December, at Charing Cross Hospital, he died as a result of having his thigh smashed, after being trampled by a police horse. His death was an embarrassment to the police but a victory for the Radical movement. Tens of thousands turned out for his funeral, including William Morris and Annie Besant. A month later, another participant in the riot died – William Curwin, a stonemason from Deptford. His funeral was also turned into a celebration of the Radical cause. The anniversaries of 'Bloody Sunday' were marked for some years to come, but otherwise, the day's violence had changed little, except perhaps to harden attitudes on both sides. Warren became a hero of the middle classes, but his triumph was shortlived: in the following year the police were unable to catch the murderer known as Jack the Ripper and faced great hostility from all sides. Warren resigned his post in November 1888, having attacked the Civil Service in print, contrary to departmental rules.

Conclusion

Most of the riots described here had been of short duration, involving a relatively small number of people – the exception being the Gordon Riots. In most, the forces of law and order, once roused, were effective in restoring order; although, of course, in two cases, they were arguably the cause of turning a peaceful political protest into a violent encounter. London can often be a violent city – as can many others – but the instances of mass public disturbances are rare, which is probably why they cause so much alarm. Rarer were the Jacobite threat of 1745 and the bombings of the nineteenth century. The first was greeted with defiance and a demonstration of solidarity with the status quo. The second was met with sympathy among Londoners and a rallying of many Irish Londoners to pledge their loyalty to the Queen and against the terrorists.

Chapter 4

The World Wars 1914–1945

*The man who says he doesn't mind being bombed or shelled is either a
liar or a maniac.*[1]

Unlike many capital cities in the last two centuries – such as Paris, Berlin and
Washington – London has never been attacked by an invading army: at least,
not from the land or sea. Scientific advances, however, provided a new means
of attacking London – aerial assault. The best known of these was the Blitz
of 1940–1941 during Second World War. Well known, too, are the flying bomb
and missile attacks that followed. Lesser known, are those that occurred in the
First World War. All, however, caused devastation in London, and this chapter
examines how Londoners reacted to such unprecedented calamities.

First World War Bombing 1915–1918
The First World War began in August 1914. Despite the German aim of a
swift victory, their plans were thwarted. By the end of the year, the German
army and its opponents, on both Western and Eastern Fronts, were stuck
in trenches and the war seemed to have reached a stalemate. Given allied
naval superiority and victories in the world outside Europe, matters looked
unpromising for Germany. Therefore, in May 1915, the Germans decided to
attack London from the air, in order to destroy the nerve centre of the British
economy. It was thought that if the City – the financial heart of the country,
replete with the Stock Exchange, the Bank of England and numerous warehouses – could be knocked out, then a victory for Germany would be all the
closer. Initially, on 5 May 1915, the decision was taken to restrict bombing to
the part of London east of the Tower. But lobbying from the High Command
persuaded the Kaiser to sign an order in July for unrestricted aerial attacks
anywhere on London, apart from the royal palaces and historic buildings –
though how the latter were to avoid being damaged was unclear.

At first, the Germans attacked London with zeppelins – sausage-shaped
airships capable of dropping bombs on the city. Zeppelins had been anticipated
by the British as a potential threat at the outset of war. Aerial gun defences
and aircraft squadrons were placed in readiness on the Thames estuary. The

latter carried men armed with rifles, which fired incendiary bullets, causing the German airships to explode. From autumn 1914, however, zeppelin bases were attacked by British aircraft. Nevertheless, in 1916 there was Parliamentary criticism of the inadequacy of London's air defences. In all, there were eleven zeppelin raids on London, in which a total of 522 people were killed in the bombing, and treble that number injured. Material losses were limited, except in a few raids, and in one case the damage amounted to £1.5 million (around £90 million in modern terms).

It is worth noting that air-raids took place against other English towns and cities (as well as Allied cities like Antwerp, Paris and Warsaw), though it was London that bore the brunt of the attacks.

Apart from the zeppelins, there were raids by aircraft, but compared with the Second World War, on a relatively small scale: two attacks by single aircraft in 1916 and several in 1917–1918, involving about twenty aircraft (Gothas). These raids killed 670 people and injured 1,960 others, mostly in the City and the East End. Yet contemporaries were not to know that these attacks would be dwarfed by those of the later conflict, so this new style of warfare was an unpleasant novelty.

Perversely, however, many were struck by the splendour of the spectacle these flying machines presented and were eager to view their progress. John Buchan's fictional hero, Richard Hannay, describes such a raid in the novel, *Mr Standfast*, set in 1918:

> Then I realized that something very odd was happening. There was a dull sound like the popping of corks of flat soda water bottles. There was a humming, too, from very far up in the skies [...] The drone grew louder, and, looking up, I could see the enemy planes flying in a beautiful formation, very leisurely as it seemed, with all London at their mercy.[2]

The writer Arnold Bennett (1867–1931) recalled accompanying friends to the top of the Waldorf Hotel on 11 September 1915 to watch the progress of two zeppelins. He wrote that the machines were 'Fairy-like [...] [the] spectacle agreed to be superb. Noise of bombs agreed to be absolutely intimidating. And noise of our guns merely noise of pop-guns'. One raid was described by Vera Brittain's aunt, who wrote: 'the noise of the bombs & the aerial guns was terrific, past imagining unless heard'. A patient in a hospital described one thus:

> one of the zeppelins, which looked like a great silver cigar in a luminous cloud, which was the smoke of the shrapnel from our

The Tower of London, from which victims were plucked in the Peasants' Revolt of 1381. (*Reg Eden's Collection*)

Lambeth Palace, where the Archbishop of Canterbury, Gilbert Sheldon, resided during the Plague of 1665. (*Author's Collection*)

Paul de la Roche's painting of the execution of Lady Jane Grey who was the focus of unrest in London in 1553. (*Author's Collection*)

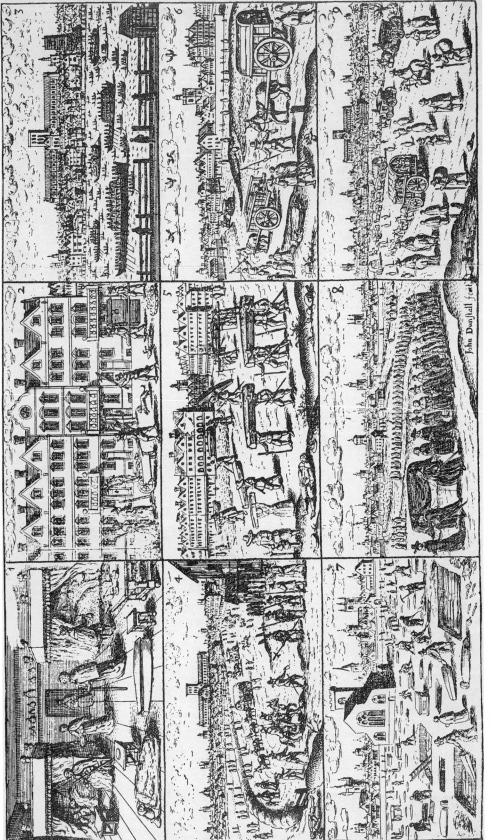

Plague victims in 1665. (*Museum of London*)

Samuel Pepys (1633–1703), chronicler of the Plague and Fire.
(*Museum of London*)

The Monument, built to commemorate the Great Fire of London.
(*Paul Lang's Collection*)

Scene of rioting during the Gordon Riots, 1780. (*Museum of London*)

The Bank of England, attacked during the Gordon Riots, 1780. (*Reg Eden's Collection*)

Horace Walpole, a keen observer of the London scene in the eighteenth century. (*Author's Collection*)

Trafalgar Square, 1890s, scene of rioting in 1887. (*Author's Collection*)

Zeppelin brought down at Potters Bar, 1916. (*Author's Collection*)

The end of the 'Baby-Killer', as zeppelins were known, 1916. (*Author's Collection*)

Bomb damage in High Holborn, 1940. (*Author's Collection*)

Londoners take shelter in a tube station during the Blitz. (*Taylor Library*)

A modern photograph of the site of the Druid Street bombing of 1940 in which seventy-seven people died. The event is now commemorated by a plaque. (*Taylor Library*)

London Borough of Southwark

Druid Street Arch Bombing

On October 25th 1940 a bomb fell through the railway arch killing 77 people sheltering from the air raid

Voted by the People

A captured V-2 rocket in Belgium, 1944. (*Author's Collection*)

Blenheim Crescent, scene
of rioting in 1958.
(*Author's Collection*)

Balcombe Road, scene of an
IRA siege, 1976.
(*Author's Collection*)

Scotland Yard, 2007.
(*Author's Collection*)

Memorial tablet at King's Cross
station, 2007. (*Author's Collection*)

anti-aircraft guns bursting underneath it. One of the guns was only about a mile away from the hospital, and that and the bombs made a terrific noise.

Many of the hospital patients were 'afflicted with nerves'.[3]

Meanwhile, Lady Cynthia Asquith saw the raids as an amusing diversion. On 1 June 1915 she wrote in her diary: 'I was horrified at the idea of having slept through it [the zeppelin attack]', and three months later: 'I shall never get over having missed it – it makes me furious'. However, on 13 October that year, her wish was almost granted and she wrote:

> we heard the magic word 'zeppelin'. We rushed out and found people in dramatic groups, gazing skywards. Some men there said they saw the zeppelin. Alas. I didn't! But our guns were popping away and shells bursting in the air. I felt excited pleasurably, but not the faintest tremor and I longed and longed for more to happen. Bibs was the only member of the family who had sufficient imagination to be frightened and Letty's fun was spoilt by the thought of the children.[4]

Miss Mary Coules described a similar scene in September 1915:

> bombs dropping – it makes a steady boom like cannon [...] I could hear the ack-ack shells bursting over the City. True enough, there were bright flashes all over the sky, & sharp bangs whenever a shell burst – quite a different sound from the bombs. We watched them chase the zeppelin from the west to the north-west, shells bursting around it [...] It only lasted 15 minutes, so far as we were concerned. Still, it was thrilling while it lasted.[5]

Michael MacDonagh, a journalist, described his first sight of a zeppelin on 9 September 1915:

> I saw an amazing spectacle. High in the sky was a zeppelin, picked out of the darkness by searchlights – a long, narrow object of a silvery hue. I felt like what a watcher of the skies must feel when a new planet swims into his ken, for it was my first sight of an enemy airship.[6]

Yet, as he noted in the following month, while he and others were looking upwards at the zeppelin, 'The thing of beauty had transformed herself into a hellish monster, and was pouring fire and death upon the crowded streets.'[7]

The young Evelyn Waugh recorded in his schoolboy diary in 1915:

> Alec [his elder brother] woke me up in the night at about 11 o'clock saying the zeps had come. We came downstairs and the special constable was rushing about yelling 'Lights out' and telling us the zeppelin was right overhead. We heard two bombs and then the Parliament Hill guns were going and the zep went away in their smoke cloud to do some baby-killing elsewhere.[8]

Recalling these events almost fifty years later, the now famous author recalled that the raids did not seem dangerous:

> No bomb fell within a mile of us, but the alarms were agreeable occasions when I was brought down from bed and regaled with an uncovenanted picnic. I was quite unconscious of danger, which was indeed negligible. On summer nights we sat in the garden [...] On a splendid occasion I saw one brought down, sinking very slowly in brilliant flame, and joined those who were cheering in the road outside.[9]

John Buchan describes the initial effect of the bombing:

> People in the streets were either staring at the heavens or running wildly for shelter. A motor-bus in front of me emptied its contents in a twinkling; a taxi pulled up with a jar and the driver and his fare dived into a second-hand bookshop [...] The man who says he doesn't mind being bombed or shelled is either a liar or a maniac. The London air-raid seemed to me a singularly unpleasant business.[10]

Once the novelty had worn off, and people had satisfied their curiosity regarding the appearance of the enemy aircraft, they began to react – in other words, they sought protective cover. Lady Asquith observed that 'all the traffic ceases, and the streets magically empty – the whole population swallowed up in houses.' Nevertheless, some enthusiastic spectators remained, for another contemporary account refers to 'The streets were full of excited semi-dressed people'.[11] Generally speaking, however, Londoners were learning how to react to aerial attack. Arnold Bennett described how, during a raid on 3 October 1917, 'Piccadilly emptied very fast. All the people ran out of the Park.' A few days earlier, a raid began just after he left his club, 'The buses seemed to quicken, the streets appreciably emptied. Most people hurried; I did, but a few strolled along. I was glad when I got to the Albany.' On another occasion he wrote: 'Everybody ran. Girls ran [...] However, I found that after a Turkish bath I couldn't run much in a heavy overcoat. So I walked. It seemed a long way.' It was also bad for business. Bennett recalled a proprietor of a restaurant telling him that: 'although his place was always full of a night, he had only four people on Monday night, and not a single customer on Tuesday night (fear of the raids)'.[12]

Many were terrified, Lady Asquith recording several examples. On one occasion, she wrote: 'Parlour maid came in quaking with fear, the potatoes rattling in the dish and informed us that the postman had told her the worst raid yet known was then in progress over London.' And a month later: 'poor little Martin was very frightened and refused, quite rationally, to be reassured, saying "But when they come with bombs they do kill people. They killed my papa."' There was also a rumour that the premier, Lloyd George (1860–1945), was so shaken with terror that two typists fainted at the sight, thinking some disaster had occurred.[13]

Others made money from the raids. Miss Tower wrote: 'one big wine dealer was reported to have let several of his cellars'. During the bigger air-raids of late September 1917, sandbags were on sale, ranging from a shilling to twopence each, depending on which part of London they were being sold in. Some people charged up to five shillings for a night's shelter in their property, depending on how wealthy the 'clients'. Taxi-drivers are reputed to have demanded exorbitant fares.[14]

Precautions were taken by some. Miss Tower wrote:

> People began to make preparations for zeppelin raids [...] people we knew had furnished theirs [cellars] and slept with big coats and handbags for valuables by the bedside. Most people had water or buckets of sand or fire extinguishers on every landing. We rather laughed at this at first but by degrees everyone came round to taking certain precautions.[15]

Poorer people could not take the same precautions as their social superiors. Many left the factories earlier in order to find shelter somewhere. Public parks and fields outside London were chosen as places to shelter, as well as the London Underground. But officials were scandalised: parks were supposed to be clear of the public and closed at dusk and, as for the Underground platforms, as one sign read: 'At no time must the platforms be used except by persons alighting from, entering in or waiting for trains.' Yet there was little officialdom could do. One park-keeper was shocked that people were still in his park after closing time. He complained to a constable, who explained that he could hardly arrest them all. Sensibly, he told the park-keeper to simply lock the park gates and go home. Elsewhere, ugly confrontations between police and squatters erupted, especially in the East End.[16] The Underground, however, remained the main option for shelterers. Lloyd George claimed that, following the raid of 7 July 1917:

> At the slightest rumour of approaching aeroplanes, Tubes and tunnels were packed with panic-stricken men, women and children. Every clear night the commons around London were black with refugees from the threatened metropolis.[17]

In October 1917, a quarter of a million Londoners sheltered in the Underground stations. Some clambered aboard the carriages of the Tube trains. Two such were William Bignell (1890–1970), a soldier on leave, and Alice Howard, his girlfriend. They sought sanctuary on a Tube train during a raid in 1917, when sheltering at Finsbury Park station. Unfortunately for them, the train set off and they found themselves at Hammersmith: they could only return home the following morning after paying the appropriate fare.

In two instances there was panic, leading to stampedes and deaths. One of these happened at Bishopsgate on 28 January 1918, when a rush to the shelter resulted in one man falling and others being suffocated or being pushed against the walls. Fourteen died in a similar incident at Mile End Underground station. John Buchan recorded:

> I found the Tube entrance filled with excited humanity. One stout lady had fainted, and a girl had become hysterical, but on the whole people were behaving well. Oddly enough they did not seem inclined to go down the stairs to the complete security of the Underground; but preferred rather to collect where they could still get a glimpse of the upper world, as if they were torn between fear of their lives and interest in the spectacle. That crowd gave me a good deal of respect for my countrymen. But several were badly rattled.[18]

As in the case of the parks, there was hostility towards the shelterers. One instance of this was recorded by Arnold Bennett. He recounted how:

> Very poor women and children sitting on stairs [of the Underground] (fear of raids). Also travellers in lift and lift man grumbling at them because no fear of raid, and they answering him back, and middle-class women saying to each other that if the poor couldn't keep to the regulations they ought to be forbidden the Tube as a shelter from the raid.[19]

It should be noted that no air-raid shelters were constructed during this period. Yet the public demanded that precautions be taken. In 1915, the police commissioner noted that: 'manifestations of popular opinion have occurred in favour of the total extinction of the street lighting when warning is received of an impending attack by hostile aircraft'. There were meetings of local government officials to discuss measures to be taken. It was decided that, when enemy airships or aircraft were seen, lighting in the capital would be dimmed but not wholly extinguished, for fear that utter darkness would cause panic and hinder the emergency services.[20]

Meanwhile, some fortunates simply fled the capital. Bruce Cummings, a naturalist, said that one raid left him with 'a fit of uncontrollable trembling' and the next induced a heart attack. He finally quit the capital for the safety of the countryside. Generally speaking, though, it was only the middle classes who could leave London, mostly women and children, though we do not know how many did, nor for how long. But it was noted that some factories in London employing people from the East End saw the number of employees fall, as some fled to Brighton.[21]

Some Londoners, however, refused to budge. Beatrice Webb recorded her reactions at the time, which were those of fear, followed by stoic acceptance of the danger:

> Six successive air-raids have wrecked the nerves of Londoners, with the result of a good deal of panic even among the well-to-do and the educated. The first two nights I felt myself under the sway of foolish fear. My feet were cold and my heart pattered its protest against physical danger. But the fear wore off, and by Monday night's raid I had recovered self-possession.[22]

For many Londoners, however, the only shelter was their own home. On 19 February 1918 Michael MacDonagh wrote that he, his wife, and his wife's sister:

> sat in our little kitchen during the raid. We have ceased going into the poky coal cellar, for it really affords no additional safety to compensate for its discomfort [...] Like millions of other Londoners – average people, simple, natural unheroic – who are in the same situation as we are tonight, the idea that a raider might come our way and drop a bomb on our house is so utterly preposterous – the chances against it running to millions – to be entertained for a moment. Why should the raider single us out of all vast London for a visit? Why indeed? Ridiculous![23]

A similar attitude was voiced by the Lord Chancellor on 31 January 1918 when the debate at the House of Lords was interrupted by bombers overhead: 'It must never be said that the peers of this ancient Realm were compelled to cease their deliberations on public affairs by a German air-raid.' And stoicism was displayed during a raid on Reuters. Miss Coules wrote: 'the office behaved splendidly. One man actually stuck to his post and worked all through it – rather than go out and watch the bombs drop'. But the office boys were allowed to go to the cellar if they wished.[24]

The epitome of coolness under fire was Lady Asquith. On 17 February 1918 she 'read Keats's letters to the accompaniment of another air-raid'. In the previous year, she described a dinner on the night of a raid:

> It was funny, sitting down calmly to dinner, with Tonks and his sister to the accompaniment of such an orchestra. They are quite blasé, having been in London for all the previous ones. The noise still exhilarates me. We stayed in the dining room – it being the most sheltered part of the house. It was a very much more desultory raid than the previous ones, going on intermittently for about three hours.

Yet even her spirits could sink and on the following day she wrote, after noting bomb damage, 'Felt tired and depressed'.[25]

Sir Henry Rider Haggard was in London during the war and on the night of a raid in October 1916 was invited down into the servants' hall in the basement, and he took his pipe and a novel. He later wrote: 'I confess I am heartily tired of zeppelins and should like some good nights' rest.'

One alleged bomb expert told Arnold Bennett that sheltering in the cellar was the worst thing to do because the bombs only exploded after they had crashed through every single floor, so that the first floor (or cellar) was not safest.[26]

During a lull in a raid on 29 January 1918, MacDonagh decided to leave his shelter and risk going home. Although he had often walked through London at night, this time it was different. There were no buses or taxis, and no itinerant street hawkers, such as coffee-stall men, roast chestnut sellers or hot potato men.

After a raid there was, naturally enough, great relief. Life went on pretty quickly, as Bennett recorded in 1915. At 10.45pm the raid began and half an hour later, he wrote that he thought it 'very strange to see motor buses going along just as usual, and a man selling fruit just as usual at corner. People spoke to each other in the street'. He added that once the all clear was sounded, the next sound was 'The footsteps of man. Then the footsteps of ten people, of twenty, of a hundred. The town was alive again'.[27]

Sometimes the airborne raiders were shot down. On 2 October 1916 a zeppelin had been hit and was in flames. If it went down on London, the destruction would have been immense. People watched its progress with keen interest. Michael MacDonagh reported:

> When at last the doomed airship vanished from sighting there arose a shout the like of which I never heard in London before – a hoarse shout of mingled execration, triumph and joy: a swelling shout that appeared to be rising from all parts of the metropolis, ever increasing in force and intensity. It was London's Te Deum for another crowning deliverance.[28]

The crowds went wild. Miss Tower wrote on 2 October 1916, when two zeppelins were hit, 'I was startled by an outburst of cheering from the crowd below'. Another observer recalled:

> The spontaneous barrage of cheering and shouting made the roar of 100,000 people at a pre-war Cup Final sound like an undertone. People danced, kissed, hugged and sang. The hysteria and the abandoned emotion were not confined to one neighbourhood [...] The crowd's reactions everywhere were described as being greater than that which celebrated the relief of Mafeking.[29]

The first airship to be shot down crashed in Potters Bar, Middlesex, 14 miles from the capital. Crowds boarded trains to visit. MacDonagh recalled that all twenty seats in his compartment were taken, and there were ten people standing. Once at Potters Bar railway station, there was another 2 miles to travel. He recorded: 'It was a joyful crowd all the same.' Some showed a morbid curiosity. One lady asked if she could see the charred and mutilated remains of the crew, 'May I go in? I would love to see a dead German.' But her request was refused. Likewise, people came from miles away to see the bomb crater at Brentford.[30]

Charities also raised money by cashing in on the raids. In September 1916 the remains of downed zeppelins, including one that had fallen near Cuffley, were displayed at the grounds of the Honourable Artillery Company in the City. The entrance fees raised £150 for the Red Cross. In the following month there was a 'Great Demand for Zeppelin Relics'. Strips of wire from the same zeppelin were sold in London by the British Red Cross – apparently, half a million were sold after the War Office gave the remnants of the zeppelin to the charity.

Reactions were sometimes ugly. The Bishop of London referred to the zeppelins as 'baby killers' after a baby was killed in an air-raid on 31 May 1915, and as we have seen, this emotive terminology was adopted by others. After houses in Streatham had been bombed on 24 September 1916, there was anger. MacDonagh recorded the scene:

> Bitter resentment against the Germans found expression among the people generally in denunciation and curses. Oh, those Huns! Harmless and defenceless citizens, far away from the Front, liable to be killed in their beds by a marauder in the skies who steals upon them unawares; whose presence they realise only when their homes are tumbling about them in ruins. 'How dastardly!' 'Barbarians!' 'Infamous!' 'Blast and damn them!'[31]

More violent reactions also occurred. Following the first zeppelin attack, Londoners retaliated in the only way open to them. They attacked the shops of Germans long resident in England, just as their predecessors in 1666 had molested Dutch and Frenchmen in the wake of the Great Fire. Even long-established German shopkeepers, who had been in London for years, found themselves in danger from their former friends and customers. One German baker was only saved from serious injury by the intervention of the police. And yet, some constables were reluctant to protect the German shopkeepers and those who did were verbally abused by the crowds. Quite what the German shopkeepers thought of all this is another matter – they were probably shocked that people they had known for years could attack them because of the actions of their fellow countrymen.

The mood could change, however, once a raid was over.

For example, one journalist noted that: 'Last night there was nervousness and exasperation; today there was curiosity. What I saw was like a fair attended by holidaymakers.' Lady Asquith went to see bomb damage at Lincoln's Inn, denying the accusation from a friend that her excitement was due to boredom.

The bombing on the night of 9 September 1915 killed nine people travelling on one bus in the City and injured another eleven on that doomed form of transport. Over half a million pounds' (approximately 30 million in modern terms) worth of damage to property had occurred and another twenty-nine people had died and 113 others had been injured, as well as the bus casualties on 9 September. Yet, as Michael MacDonagh noted: 'The crowds of visitors to the extensive area of the raid were more curious than angry, I thought.' Boys and girls, on seeing shop windows smashed by the bombs, gathered shards of glass and pieces of shrapnel: 'There was an eager hunt for souvenirs of the raid.' Occasionally, penknives had to be used to prise out such items from pavements and walls. When the relics had been carried away, there was applause from onlookers. Some thought the damage minimal. Miss Coules wrote, after a visit to see the aftermath of a raid in September 1915: 'Considering that there were three zeppelins, it really isn't very extensive.'[32]

Nevertheless, the civilian authorities did little to lessen potential danger, leading to some displays of animosity on the part of disgruntled locals. That said, some public buildings were protected by sandbags, but air-raid shelters were not constructed, despite public pleas. Instead, civilians were told to take shelter in their own homes or in public buildings. MacDonagh recorded on the occasion of London's first daylight raid (7 July 1917):

> There was deep exasperation at the audacity, 'the damned impudence', of the Germans. Did they not show how they despise our defences by twice coming over in broad daylight and successfully carrying off their-raids [. . .] [a British airplane was seen overhead] [. . .] 'Give the Bosches hell – when you overtake them.' Derisive laughter burst out, fists were shaken at him.[33]

Miss Tower noted:

> People began to get very excited about the zeppelins and to blame the government for not providing better protection against them, and there were meetings to suggest air reprisals and in other ways to give valuable help to the authorities.

Retaliation was demanded. Seeing aircraft bring down a zeppelin, a Cockney news-vendor shouted: 'Now we can hit the buggers in their own bleedin' backyard.' On 2 October 1917, after seeing bomb damage, Lloyd George said: 'We shall give it all back to them, and we shall give it back very soon. We shall bomb Germany with compound interest.' The 'Welsh Wizard' always knew what to tell people, but in this case action did not match his words.[34]

Due to wartime censorship, newspapers were remarkably reticent over the bombing, so in place of hard facts, stories circulated. Miss Tower recorded, on going to work in a hospital on the night after a raid:

> all kinds of yarns and rumours were busy. An airship was reported to have been brought down on Hampstead heath, in Finsbury Park, Regent's park and at Harrow and Gravesend; in the last she was said to have fallen into the river and had been destroyed by a torpedo boat.

Another story told how a fire had been deliberately started in a factory in Wood Lane, in the City, in order to guide the bombers (a blackout was in force), but as Miss Tower commented: 'I dare say this story was not true.'[35]

The London air-raids provoked reactions. Many, at least at first, saw them as a novel spectacle – a form of entertainment. Others, however, appreciated the danger. Although casualties were relatively light, this was a new form of warfare in which civilians were placed in deadly peril. But there was little they could do except take cover wherever they could find it or leave the capital. The German bombing campaign was not aimed directly at civilians, but the financial resources of the country – in this it failed. The last raid on London, which occurred on 19 May 1918, resulted in several losses among the attackers: six out of the eighty aircraft involved were shot down. Further aerial attacks on London were called off as being too costly.

The Blitz 1940–1941

Although the Germans continued to experiment with zeppelins as machines of war in the 1930s, their vulnerability to improved fighter aircraft made them obsolete. Although used to observe British radar defences in September 1939, they were broken up for scrap a few months later, and it was, of course, the highly developed Luftwaffe that became the aerial spearhead of the Nazi war machine. Fears of mass bombing of defenceless cities were commonplace throughout the 1930s. The devastation wrought to cities in the Spanish Civil War of 1936–1939 was fresh in the minds of many (Guernica had been destroyed by bombing in 1937). Governments believed that the civilian populations could not withstand mass aerial attack. Fiction also developed this theme – the terrifying early scenes of the film *Things to Come* depict a bombing raid that is both deadly and invulnerable to anti-aircraft defences. Panic, riot and the breakdown of civil government were predicted. As Stanley Baldwin (Conservative Prime Minister 1923–4, 1924–9 and 1935–7) observed: 'the bomber will always get through'. An official report of 1937 forecast that a 60-day bomber offensive on London would lead to 600,000 dead and twice that number injured. In the thriller, *Bulldog Drummond at Bay* (1935), the effects of an imagined raid are described thus:

> in the streets mobs of screaming men and women rushed frenziedly about, trampling, fighting, mad with terror. The Tube stations were full – too full; already people were being suffocated to death. And on the platforms below those in front were pushed on to the lines unable to withstand the pressure of those behind.

When there was an air-raid alarm in September 1939, John Colville, a civil servant, noted:

> It was widely believed that London would be reduced to rubble within minutes of war being declared, as recently depicted to an

alarmed populace in the film of H.G. Wells's *The Shape of Things to Come*; and it seemed that this was indeed about to happen.[36]

Many of these fears were the result of exaggerated reporting. It was said that the bombing of Rotterdam on 14 May 1940 resulted in tens of thousands of dead. Although the bombing had been severe, fatalities probably did not exceed 900. Likewise, the bombing raids in Spain and the Far East in the 1930s had been less deadly than anticipated – and reported – and had not won the war for the aggressors (the Japanese bombing of Nanking had in fact stiffened Chinese resistance).

Thus, with the outbreak of the Second World War in September 1939, the role of the Luftwaffe was seen to be of paramount importance. Its aircraft played a crucial role in the defeat of Poland in the first month of war, as well as that of France the following year. Given the newly formed Churchillian government's refusal to surrender, the Luftwaffe's deployment against London was only a matter of time.

Bombing during the Second World War was on a far wider and more deadly scale than during the First. Although there had been some bombs dropped on London in August 1940, during the Battle of Britain, once the Luftwaffe switched from bombing RAF bases to blasting British towns, the Blitz began in earnest.

Most bombing raids took place at night, in an effort to minimise air-crew losses. The first major bombing of London occurred on 7 September (perpetrated by 320 aircraft) and attacks continued until 10 May 1941. Within this period, 18,800 tons of bombs were dropped over a total of 57 raids. This resulted in over 20,000 deaths and more than a million homes being damaged or destroyed. The worst night of the bombing was the last – 10 May 1941 – with over 1,400 fatalities, 12,000 made homeless and 5,000 homes destroyed. These were shocking sights to witness even in the aftermath. According to one diarist:

> Mr Raphael said when he went to Moorfields and saw Raphael House a shell & the scene of devastation around he broke down and I can well believe it enough to break anyone's heart.[37]

Londoners sheltered from the bombs in a variety of ways. Some simply stayed at home – sleeping under the stairs, in the cellar or in cupboards. Mrs Florence Turtle, a middle-class, middle-aged housewife of Wimbledon, wrote on 9 September 1940: 'I stood in the broom cupboard under the stairs & wondered if the next moment would be our last.' Some Londoners, perhaps a quarter, had Anderson shelters in their back gardens – steel shelters that could sleep six and were proof against anything other than a direct hit. Others slept in communal shelters. Although it was officially disapproved of, many sheltered in the Underground stations. Some 79 stations sheltered about 177,000 people (less than 4 per cent of the population). The shelters were dry and well lit and the noise of the air-raids was all but inaudible. Others fled the capital: many – perhaps 12,000–15,000 – seeking sanctuary in the caves at Chislehurst. Most (about 60 per cent), however, ignored such alternative accommodation and slept in their own beds.[38]

Although time in the shelters was unpleasant, at least it saved lives. Len Jones, who lived in Poplar, later recalled:

> The shelter was brick and concrete built, and it was lifting and moving, rolling almost as if it was a ship on rough sea. And the suction and blasts coming in and out of this steel door, which was smashing backwards and forwards, bashed us around against the walls. The extent of injuries at that stage was just abrasions really, the shoulders and the chest getting crushed against the wall, or across the floor. The worst part was the poor little kids; they were so scared, they were screaming, crying, clutching at their parents.[39]

Conditions in large-scale shelters, whether official or unofficial, were often appalling. Washing facilities and lavatories were non-existent. A few buckets might be there if you were lucky. Thousands sheltered under the railway arches in Stepney. Nina Hibbin wrote:

> The first time I went in there, I had to come out, I felt sick. You just couldn't see anything, you could just smell the fug, the over-whelming stench. It was like the Black Hole of Calcutta. There were thousands and thousands of people laying head to toe, all along the bays and with no facilities [. . .] The place was like a hell-hole, it was an outrage that people had to live in these conditions.

Even family shelters were not ideal, as Mrs Turtle wrote in 1941: 'down to the shelter to rest. Camp beds, blankets and eiderdowns. Plenty warm enough, but so terribly stuffy. Did not sleep at all until 3.15.'[40]

Yet there were some compensations. People often thought that they were safer in large numbers, though this was not always justified. But they did give a great boost to community solidarity. Networks built up, people would chat, tell jokes and sing songs. Small things, maybe, but they helped. In a Tube station, Mary Price sat on the stairs and a man later approached her. She recalled:

he said 'I can't let you sit there.' And I was amazed that he said: 'You take my place on the platform.' I was amazed to think that he would do that, and I went down and took his place. But that's the sort of thing that happened, people would do anything for each other.[41]

But life during the Blitz was not all one of good neighbourliness and comradeship. Class conflict raised its head during the initial stages. Because the East End and poorer parts of London were, at first, more affected by bombing than the more prosperous western parts of the capital, residents in the former were doubly envious of the latter. They heard about deep and comfortable air-raid shelters under hotels and exclusive department stores. Some rich people were thought to look down on the poorer citizens and this was also resented. On one occasion, nightclub revellers jeered at some firemen who were taking a break. When Lord Portman's house was on fire, Maurice Wood recalled an ARP man asking if anyone was inside, and when the answer was in the negative, said 'Let it burn then.'[42]

Certainly, for some in high society, life was not at all bad. On 9 November, Evelyn Waugh – now an officer in the Marines – attended a cocktail party and had champagne, oysters and cigars. He wrote: 'It was not all what the neutrals imagine life in London to be like.' Life went on. Colville recorded on 22 October: 'Rode on a splendid chestnut of Louis Greig's in Richmond Park, where a thick mist made riding hazardous owing to the large number of bomb-craters and unexploded bombs.' In the following month, he recorded:

> One can be quite comfortable these days in spite of the bombs. I had a bath in the p.m.'s bath at No. 10, and then sat in his downstairs room in my dressing gown, reading *Madame Bovary* and drinking some delicious brown ale provided by Barker.[43]

Hilda Neal was told by a bus driver that the East End was left to the bombs and that the government only put up barrage balloons when the West End was in danger. Her reaction to this was the following observation: 'I could see he was a born grouse and troublemaker.' Likewise, some thought that such agitation and references to 'those parasites at Buckingham Palace' was the work of German agents. There was even a story about such an agent, whose corpse was later found in a watery bomb crater – although, apparently, he had not died by drowning.[44]

Mrs Turtle recorded her mixed views about working-class responses to the bombing in 1940–1941. On 9 September 1940, she noted sympathetically, at Liverpool Street Station: 'Crowds of people trying to get away from London.

Eastenders with their pitiful little bundles in cardboard boxes.' Yet in the following year, on 28 May, she was severe in recording:

> Going home via Holborn Tube at 9.10 pm I saw some of the shelterers waiting to go down; they were a shocking-looking lot, scarcely the back-bone of the nation – funny how the lowest types are always the most anxious to protect themselves and survive.[45]

Yet a change in German bombing helped create a temporary social unity. Richer parts of London, such as Kensington and Belgravia, were bombed. So was Buckingham Palace and the Queen famously remarked: 'I'm glad we've been bombed. It makes me feel I can look the East End in the face.' Mrs Uttin recorded on 22 January 1941: 'this war affects us all – even Buckingham Palace was not immune from the raids for it was bombed in daylight whilst the King and Queen were in residence.' Mrs Turtle recorded the fact that the palace had been attacked in her diary, too. On a royal visit to a bombed district, a woman enquired about how many guns were defending the East End and another answered on the King's behalf: 'Give 'im time, dearie, E's the right sort. I don't suppose there's no more guns round the Pallis [*sic*].'[46]

The Prime Minister was also a source of inspiration for many. Mrs Rose Uttin, a middle-aged housewife of Wembley, also spoke with admiration for Churchill: 'When Mr Churchill took office he said he could offer us nothing but "blood, and sweat, toils and tears" – how right he is – and how lost we would have been without him.' A socialist recalled, seeing Churchill: 'with a cigar sticking out of his fat pink face' after the bombing on the Columbia market, 'a few people cheered and even I felt like cheering'. On another occasion, Frank Lewey, socialist Mayor of Stepney, claimed that an old lady said: 'I bet old 'Itler daren't go among 'is folk like this. They'd pull him to bits, some of them.'[47]

But there was also unity among many. Mr Goodall, a Yorkshire warden in Hammersmith in 1944, recorded:

> it's a happy post, of 34 wardens, each and everyone good friends, quarrelling, rows, nasty gossip are not known here – there is no snobbery, doctors, dentists and other professional men are here on the same footing with the bricklayer, carpenter or coal roundsmen, all are out to help one another and to stand by one another in all dangers.

Dr Frank Cockett, an Australian, observed that the raids 'were doing more to knit England together than anything else could,' while a journalist, Mr Favell wrote: 'It was amazing that people talked to one another. They opened up amazingly about how they felt, thought and what they thought.'[48]

This co-operation took many forms. Once hitch-hiking had been hardly respectable. But with the disruption of public transport due to the bombing, it became fashionable and patriotic. Neighbours pooled resources and their time in fire-watching duties and setting up improvised field kitchens. Air-raid wardens were often useful sources of help and information – not all were the authoritarian figures portrayed in the TV comedy, *Dad's Army*.

After the initial shock of the bombing, 'Business as usual' became the motto for many Londoners. Shopkeepers would proudly open even if their shop had suffered some damage – it was simply a case of 'More open than Usual'. Simply getting to work led to a sense of pride for many.

However, some fled the capital. Gladys Strelitz recalled:

> The day after, well, we came out of the crypt and everybody was fleeing for their lives because it was still blazing. And we got the children and we knew we had to run for it like everybody else was running out of London. You had to escape, so we just managed to get into a baker's van that took us to the station. And we decided to go to Maidenhead and take the children there.[49]

Yet those who quit were not necessarily downhearted. The Chief Constable for Berkshire wrote that refugees from London 'are in no way deterred in their determination to see things through'.[50]

The first air-raid caught London unawares. The emergency services had no experience of dealing with crises on such a scale: first-aid posts were swamped with the walking wounded, ambulances had difficulty in negotiating the bomb-cratered roads, and the blazes at the dockyards were out of control. There was a sense of horror, helplessness and shock at seeing so much death and devastation. The emergency services did their best, however, and exit routes for dockland communities were kept open. Rescue squads worked at freeing those trapped by falling rubble – or digging out dead bodies.

As the press was censored, the effects of the raids, in terms of destruction and death, were concealed from the public. But this did not necessarily assist morale. People could see the damage with their own eyes as they moved about London. As a civil defence commissioner noted: 'frank explanation is what the public want and expect. Without it they feel that something is being hidden from them'.[51]

As the Blitz continued, the efficiency of the emergency services increased. There were about 25,000 men in the London fire service (most of them part-time or auxiliary, as opposed to a relatively small number of regular firemen) and they fought fires night after night. For those with daytime jobs, this was a double burden. But most did not shirk such dangerous duties. This involved much danger: not only from bombs, but from falling masonry, poisonous fumes, dehydration and many other dangers. Why did they do it? For many it was better to be doing something positive rather than passively sheltering from the bombs. For some it gave their lives excitement and purpose away from humdrum jobs. This was helped by a great sense of co-operation and mutual dependence. As Bill Ward, an auxiliary fireman recalled:

> Well, you knew you were both in the same boat. If he died, you died. If he lived, you lived. Everyone depended on everyone else. So there was great comradeship there. You knew that every man there was going to try to look after you and keep you safe, and you'd do the same for them.[52]

Other people, both men and women, had similar experiences in different services. Many women worked in the ambulance and nursing services. June Buchanan drove an ambulance in the Blitz and recalled:

> We all just did what we had to do. I'd often find myself carrying the dead and injured on stretchers into the ambulance and rushing them back to the hospital along the blacked-out streets. I just took it in my stride. The bombs would be falling all around, but you felt better out doing something to help rather than waiting for them to drop on you.[53]

The emergency services helped maintain the morale of fellow Londoners simply by doing their best throughout the crisis. The everyday things in life suddenly acquired a greater importance. For example, a cup of tea was often the first thing people needed when they returned home after a raid.

There were mixed reactions among civilians towards the bombing. Waugh wrote this of his parents: 'My father fears nothing but my mother is rather more disturbed.' John Colville wrote of his parents' departure from London:

> Mother [. . .] said at breakfast that if one looked on all this as ordinary civilian life it was indeed hellish, but if one thought of it as a siege then it was certainly one of the most comfortable in history.[54]

Some showed indifference to the potential danger. Henry St John (1911–1979), a civil servant, was travelling from Southall to work by trolleybus in September 1940 and recorded:

> We were passing Viaduct Field when the conductor indicated that there was a raid, and the sirens shrieked as we ascended the incline to

Hanwell Broadway. A man continued to clean the window of a shop in Ealing Broadway.[55]

On another occasion, after leaving his house during a raid, a man returned to fetch his clothes brush – personal appearance counting more than personal safety.

But being under fire was not a pleasant experience. Colville wrote on 22 September, 'I saw the house topple over sideways. It was nightmarish, and with our tails between our legs we crept downstairs to the dining room'. On another occasion he noted that incendiary bombs dropped 10 yards from where he threw himself to the ground – and later admitted to being 'Somewhat shaken'. Mr A.K. Goodlet (1900–1956), a fire-watcher at Dagenham, wrote on 5 September:

> For the first time, this war, too, I have come under bomb fire and I must say it is anything but a pleasant sensation. We had two big ones drop on the marshes quite close, and they made a horrid noise coming down.[56]

Yet Colville was also curious, as was Pepys during the Great Fire of 1666 or Waugh during the First World War. He wrote, on 22 September, on seeing the bombing over London:

> Nothing could have been more beautiful and the searchlights inter-laced at certain points on the horizon, the star-like flashes in the sky where shells were bursting, the light of distant fires, all added to the scene. It was magnificent and terrible [...] Never was there such a contrast of natural splendour and human vileness. Later thick palls of smoke rose from the Embankment where bombs had fallen on Dolphin Square – and it went on all night long.[57]

Similarly, Goodlet wrote on 23 August:

> Had quite an exciting night last night. At about 2 the searchlights and the sirens began and I saw my first German aircraft of the war. Very soon after that there came the vivid flashes of bombs, and up in the sky (a beautiful clear, moonlit one) there were the vivid tulip-like flashes of the bursting shells.[58]

More prosaically, Mrs Turtle recorded on 13 March 1941:

> I was just in bed and the bombers dropped some heavy luggage so got up in my dressing gown and we all looked out. We could see fires Earlsfield way.[59]

The Blitz failed in its efforts to sap morale. Colville noted on 24 November that 'The Germans have apparently learned they cannot break our spirits by fear and are concentrating their night efforts on industry.' An extract from the letter of an East End Jew, which was noted by the Censorship Report in December 1940, read:

> It is terrible here at night – every night [. . .] Death rains down from the Clouds [. . .] the raids, the machine-gunning, it is murder. The English are not so highly-strung as we. They do not seem to mind until they actually see some of their own family killed in front of their noses. Then, instead of being frightened or praying, they say 'Damn those bloody bastards.'[60]

Resentment towards the German aggressor was marked (one Londoner believing that anti-German prejudice was greater than later racial prejudice). Goodlet referred to the German bombers as 'the swine' on at least two occasions. Although he occasionally complained about his work, referring to a watch on 19 November as 'rather beastly', this was more because it was very early in the morning and his health was not the best. Mrs Turtle wanted revenge on the Germans. In January 1941, she wrote: 'May God curse those thrice blasted Nazi Germans.' Not all agreed with such sentiments, as she wrote in May:

> When people get sentimental over the poor Germans all being mothers' sons etc., I think of the 30,000 men, women and children [in Rotterdam] all butchered by the Huns – a totally undefended town. May God curse them.[61]

The government had been concerned that mass panic might break out and that civilian morale would collapse due to the aerial bombing. This did not occur. After the first shock of the bombing, Londoners got on with life and work. The 'myth' of the Blitz was played up for public consumption, both at home and abroad, but it was only a little exaggerated, not totally invented. Mass Observation reports and secret Home Office reports indicate that courage prevailed. At the end of 1940, Churchill telegraphed Roosevelt thus:

> when I visited the still burning ruins today the spirit of the Londoners was as high as in the first days of then indiscriminate bombing in September.[62]

Why was morale so high, despite the bombing and the gloomy international situation of 1940–1941? The fact that casualties were far fewer than predicted –

and feared – was one factor. Anarchy had been expected but, despite death raining down, it had not materialised. Rationing ensured Londoners had an adequate, if monotonous, diet and helped foster a feeling of solidarity amid the hardships of war. Meanwhile, London's sheer scale was a source of strength and resilience – a raid on a small town would completely devastate it, but a raid on London only damaged part of it. All, therefore, was not lost. Churchill observed that London was like a great prehistoric dinosaur and could withstand much damage. The fact that the onslaught was steady helped people accustom themselves to it: less sleep was lost as the bombing went on.

It should be mentioned, however, that the Blitz also provided an opportunity for petty crime: robbery, looting and pilfering were rife. Frank Whipple, a reserve policeman, recalled:

> There was a terrible lot of looting. You'd find bent wardens, heavy rescue men, even police doing looting. People were like vultures, going into bombed outhouses and shops and they'd even take rings and valuables off dead bodies. We would have to accompany them to the mortuaries to stop that happening.[63]

When the Café de Paris nightclub was bombed in March 1941, looters stole jewellery from the dead and injured. Gladys Strelitz returned to her home after it had been bombed and recalled, 'people had been in and looted my home and all the bed linen and everything was stolen and, well, we were full of despair.' Killers also had increased opportunities. Gordon Cummins, known as the 'Black-Out Ripper', killed several women before being caught; and John Reginald Christie, who worked in civil defence, began his career as a serial killer at this time.[64]

The impact of the bombing lasted long after the bombs had been dropped and the dead had been buried. The widespread destruction of domestic property was just as difficult to live with. The supply of basic utilities such as gas, water and electricity, was often disrupted or cut off, leaving some Londoners unable to cook or wash. At first, people could make do with temporary expedients like making fires or cooking from wood. Voluntary groups, such as the Salvation Army, also did their best to help, running mobile kitchens.

Yet in themselves, these were not enough to cope with the widespread damage the bombing had caused. It was the local authorities who had to deal with the housing difficulties many of their residents were enduring. Unfortunately, some clung to outmoded policies inadequate for so grave a crisis. Homelessness affected about a quarter of a million people by October 1940. Some people lodged with relatives or friends, but this resulted in overcrowding. Empty houses were requisitioned and homeless families relocated there. Some were evacuated.

These difficulties led to resentment and anger at the alleged indifference and incompetence of the municipal authorities. This could lead to collective action pressing for change. Committees were formed, demanding action. Eventually, in November 1940, these requests were dealt with as the question of civilian morale was important. Increased government intervention and increased funding resulted in better air-raid protection and better feeding facilities. Communal shelters were improved, with proper bedding and toilets. Although these measures were not perfect, they did improve life for many Londoners. Community spirit flourished as Rene Eary recalled:

> You got a real community going after it was organised better. Until then everyone had been shifting around and you didn't hardly know anyone. But now you had a regular spot with the same bunks every night, and the people around you became like regular neighbours.[65]

Life in communal shelters became convivial. It was no longer a case of sheltering from the bombs. People took part in group activities, such as dressmaking, debating clubs and drama. Snacks and drinks could be bought at a cheap rate. Entertainment was sometimes organised and on Sundays there was hymn singing. People did more now than simply survive.

By the time of the last and most deadly raid of the Blitz – 10 May 1941 – London and Londoners were better equipped than ever to deal with it. Emily Eary noted:

> the whole of London seemed to be on fire. We'd been down the Tube all night, but when we came out in the morning, we had to run through fires which were raging both sides of the streets. And there was hot falling embers pouring down on us. But we weren't as terrified as we used to be because by then, you see, we had got bunks down the Tube, and we had a place that was sort of secure for us.[66]

Some Londoners with a sense of history were reflective. Mrs Uttin compared the bombing with the great disaster of the Fire of 1666, writing on 29 December 1940:

> the night of the second fire of London – just the difference between the two being the deliberate firing of London by the Huns – now perhaps London and I mean the City will be built as Sir Christopher Wren planned after the first Fire with wide streets [...] Pepys in his diary of 1666 said of the first fire: 'it is the complete destruction of

London and so with a sad heart home to bed.' Not so with us – we had to wait until the last Hun plane had gone.[67]

We know less about children's experiences during the Blitz: after all, many had been evacuated. Very young children, such as Mike Hall, growing up in Greenford, were able to treat the dangers posed as part of a game. Mike recalled:

> I enjoyed the war. That is a terrible thing to write but as a small boy it was an exciting time. You didn't know what would happen from one day to the next. Searchlights lit the night sky. I didn't know, and I'm glad I didn't know, that some of those descending trails of flame were being fuelled by living, screaming human beings.

Mike recalled having to shelter with his classmates when bombs fell during lessons, but such were the stories told by his teacher in the shelter that they were aggrieved the bombing was over and real lessons had to begin again.[68]

Older children, such as Roy Bartlett of south Ealing, were more aware of the gravity of the situation. During the initial bombing he wrote that 'It is difficult now, to convey the constant feeling of terror and apprehension that everyone felt in those early stages, relieved only by intermittent welcome snatches of sleep', but 'Incredibly however, we gradually got used to it all and a revised pattern of life developed'. Although Roy described that 'I experienced the full horror of warfare, being allowed a quick glance out of the shelter doorway,' he added, 'It is strange really, but I do not recall being frightened. Perhaps the sudden awful reality was too much for a young lad to comprehend midst all the excitement, should that be the descriptive word.'[69]

What was important about Londoners' reaction to the Blitz was what did not happen. There was no panic, no civil disorder and no demands for peace to be made with Germany. Had there been, then the course of the war after 1941 would have been much different. With Britain out of the fight, any American involvement would have been less effective and the whole of Europe might have then been either neutral or under the subjugation of Nazi Germany. Londoners played a great role not only in British but also in global history.

The Missile Attacks, 1944–1945

With the end of the Blitz, the focus of the war in Europe shifted to the Eastern Front as Hitler and his allies moved against the Soviet Union. There were few air-raids on London in 1942–1943 and although 569 people were killed in occasional raids, this was minimal when compared with the casualties of the Blitz. There was a resurgence of bombing in the spring of 1944 – the 'Little Blitz' – but after that, London was granted a respite. But not for long.

The end of the Second World War must have seemed in sight in early June 1944, with the successful D-Day landings in northern France, while the might of the Soviet Union pushed the German army westwards. For the people of London, there was, however, one final ordeal. It was on the evening of 13 June that the first wave of V-1 missiles – pilotless monoplanes packed with explosives, which came to be known as 'flying bombs', 'buzz bombs' or 'doodlebugs' – were launched at Britain. Of the twenty-seven launched, four reached London, killing two people in Bethnal Green. V-1s (officially designated F2G-76 by the German High Command) flew at 390 miles per hour. Thousands of such bombs were launched in subsequent months and were especially deadly in the first two to three months. The first two months of this bombardment saw 2,224 flying bombs hit London. These killed 5,126 people and the total reported London casualties were 45,821, of which 14,712 were serious injuries. About 17,000 houses had been destroyed, mostly in South London. A fresh wave of evacuation took place, with a million people leaving London. One of the worst single incidents occurred on 18 June, when 120 people were killed during a service at the Guards' Chapel. Unlike the Blitz, all these attacks could take place in daylight as well as night-time. There was no respite brought about by dawn. Yet the V-1s could be shot down and many were. The flying bomb attacks came largely to an end in September 1944 as the bomb-sites in Holland and northern France were overrun and destroyed. Surprise was one reaction to the 'doodlebugs'. Roy Bartlett recalled:

> I was out with my friend Ken after school when the Air Raid sirens sounded. 'What's that all about – must be a mistake,' surely Jerry was far too busy to make some random attack on London. 'Ignore it, it will go away.' It did, the All-Clear sounded. 'Told you so, some silly bugger pressed the wrong button.' A few minutes later we were not so sure, the alert sounded again. What is going on?[70]

The first wave of attacks caught Londoners by surprise. William Bignell, aged sixteen, was living with his parents in Hornsey and recollects:

> Suddenly one Sunday night there was gunfire in the night, and not directed gunfire as it would have been against an aeroplane, and we hadn't been in the shelters [...] then we heard a big crash. I remember mother, father and I getting in to the place in the house which was safest; in the hall and waited there [...] We could not think what had happened [...] Nobody knew.[71]

The common experience of the V-1s was summed up by Mr Goodall, writing that after the alert sounded 'then in the distance a faint rumble gradually developing into the sound of some low approaching plane, louder, louder then with a roar it flies overhead – or – it explodes, and a sharp rumble of falling masonry'. Similarly, a young girl in Bow later recalled: 'The engine stopped, then there was a sound of whistling [...] and the next thing was a tremendous bang and the front windows came in.'[72]

There was a different atmosphere in 1944 than there had been four years previously. Colville commented: 'London seems disturbed by the raids and less ebullient than in 1940–1.' One Londoner wrote: 'Are we never to be free of damage or death? Surely five years is long enough for any town to have to suffer?' Vera Hodgson observed: 'The atmosphere in London has changed [...] Apprehension is in the air.' A West Hampstead woman, whose home had been bombed, was asked shortly afterwards by a journalist to pose giving a V for victory sign and told them: 'I refused and my daughter was not in the mood to comply.'[73]

Reactions were different to what they had been in 1940–1941 because Londoners were exhausted after the dangers, fears and privations of war and rationing. This was especially the case because, with the D-Day landings, victory seemed so close. Expectations of a swift end to the war were cruelly disappointed in a most violent manner. Once-popular government ministers, such as Herbert Morrison, the Home Secretary, were blamed for this state of affairs. But in reality, short of destroying the rocket-launching sites, there was little the government could do.

The swiftness of the V-1 rendered air-raid warnings ineffectual, London's sirens wailing too late or not at all. Eventually, they seemed to shriek all the time, leaving Londoners with the feeling that death was ever present. Charles Draper recalled: 'You never knew when one was going to get you.' The impersonal nature of the bombs themselves added another irrational fear. Odette Lesley stated:

> The doodlebugs were so much more terrifying than anything that had come along up till that time because they were supernatural, they were uncanny, they were almost science fiction [...] You accepted a plane with a man in it, you couldn't accept something that was automatic.

The sense of the inhuman mechanical menace was summed up by a character from Evelyn Waugh's *Unconditional Surrender*, who likened the V-1s to 'enormous, venomous insects [...] as impersonal as the plague'.[74] Consequently, people felt more powerless than during the Blitz. Mr Jory, who lived in a flat near Brixton Hill in South London, wrote:

> We seemed to have no answer, and it was obvious if something effective was not quickly done, there would be a considerable panic, exodus on quite the biggest scale since the Blitz began.

Housewives isolated at home lacked the support and camaraderie of women who worked in the factories. The Morrison shelters were widely used, but these also increased the sense of isolation that communal shelters did not engender.[75] There was also the problem of the lack of information due to press censorship. It was noted in the summer that:

> People in target areas and elsewhere, are critical of official and press accounts which appear to tone down the raids and the damage they cause. People ask for less secrecy and more true information.

It was felt that if people knew the dangers they were in, they would be less afraid because otherwise they imagined far worse risks than was actually the case.[76] Yet some of the earlier stoicism was still there. Mr Jory wrote in his diary:

> This week we record the coming of the pilotless plane, which Goebbels and Co. are busily proclaiming as one of the first of Hitler's secret weapons which will ultimately bring us to our knees. A week's intimate experience of this secret leaves us slightly bloody, but unbowed and he will have to try something a lot better that that.[77]

Crowds continued to attend cinemas, theatres and concerts, despite the bombing. *Gone with the Wind* still played to packed houses. A gunner recalled attending a recital at the National Gallery. The violinist was playing one of Bach's pieces, when the audience could hear the sound of a V-1 approaching. Despite the tension, the violinist continued, the beauty of the melody contrasting with the droning menace overhead. As the flying bomb passed, the audience remained still, the music seemingly taking on a triumphant quality.

The work of the emergency services was, as in the Blitz, praised. Although Mr Goodall regretted the loss of life and property, he wrote:

> there is so much to admire, the wonderful pluck and fortitude of those whose homes have vanished in a mass of death and rubble and the organisation of Rescue, Ambulance and First aid [. . .] all in full working order within a few minutes of an explosion, each man or woman to his or her job.

Sometimes, American servicemen helped in the aftermath of the raids. As an incident officer in Deptford explained:

> Having brought their own canteen, complete with lighting equipment and bulldozer they cleared the road so that our ambulance and fire brigade could get to the site [...] Without these boys we would have been in a very sorry plight.[78]

Voices of victims are relatively rare, but Elizabeth Sheppard-Jones's was one. She was badly – and permanently – disabled after being in the Guards' Chapel when it was hit. She remembered:

> I felt no pain, I was scarcely aware of the chunks of massed grey concrete that had piled on top of me, nor did I realize that this was why breathing was so difficult. My whole being was concentrated in the one tremendous effort of taking in long struggling breaths and then letting them struggle out again.[79]

Despite having his flat destroyed and him being injured, Jory could later write, of the missile attacks, 'But no one seems to be greatly upset by them – unless near them, of course'. And life went on, as Goodall wrote, despite the devastation. It had to. He wrote:

> Come the dawn, the scene of devastation can hardly be imagined, where once a dozen or more houses, stood, is only a mass of brick [...] but daily life goes on in the same old way, men and women to their work, housewives and mothers to their shopping, a dairy serving its customers today, tomorrow may not exist, but those same customers are served, with their early morning milk.

Tradesmen were as punctual as they had been during the Blitz and one milkman remembered being asked by clients to unload the crates less loudly as their nerves were affected by the bangs of the bombs. Shoppers queuing for goods did not always rush to shelter when alarms sounded.[80]

The Black Market and war-related crime increased as the conflict continued. Reported crimes rose by 50 per cent from 1938 to 1944, though this was only from 1 per cent of the population to 1.5 per cent. Many misdemeanours, however, probably went unrecorded, as petty pilfering became common. In the aftermath of the Lewisham Market bomb – one of the worst incidents of the V-1 attacks – oranges strewn all over the road, and which were usually reserved for pregnant women, 'were being picked up by people who immediately made off'. The growth of the Black Market served to decrease the communal patriotic spirit and to revive social divisions, as some people benefited from it but others, especially the poorer, did not. The Communist Party campaigned in Stepney and Poplar on the theme of social inequality, claiming that the rich were doing well out of the war, and this viewpoint gained some support.[81]

People were wearied and strained and some behaved badly. Odette Lesley noted: 'I can still remember my horror and disgust at seeing grown men avidly pushing women and children aside to get into Warren Street Tube station when the doodlebugs were coming over. I was actually shoved out of the way myself once or twice. Peoples' nerves had gone, their nerves were shot to pieces.' Mrs Uttin wrote: 'We are more than sick of it – war no nearer over than this time last year.' Self-preservation, not self-sacrifice, was the order of the day for many. No one wanted to die in the last stages of the war. Some became angry. The writer, James Lees-Milne, after seeing the damage done to the Guards' Chapel, wrote: 'I felt suddenly sick. Then a rage of fury welled inside me. For sheer damnable devilry what could be worse than that awful instrument?'[82]

Mr Bignell recalls the sense of unease that was felt, especially among adults:

> You had to live with a very increased level of anxiety all the time; sensed by adults more than someone like me [. . .] anxious all the time about it [. . .] When you left in the morning for work, you never knew whether you would see your parents again, nor them me.[83]

After nearly being killed in one incident, Mr Bignell recalls: 'It didn't trouble me as much as mum. She was absolutely shattered. It passed me by. The fact that we had missed death by one and a half seconds didn't seem to strike me. I was sixteen.'[84]

Working in the telephone exchange in Queen Victoria Street, he remembered the time when:

> Suddenly we heard a flying bomb, despite the bricked up walls, it was terribly loud [. . .] it could be us. I can remember this woman holding onto this desk [. . .] We were looking at each other, her hands gripped the desk, everyone stopped speaking [. . .] then we realised it was going away from us.[85]

On another occasion, Bignell threw himself on the ground as a flying bomb passed overhead, and a veteran of the First World War remarked: 'Of course, son, this was nothing like the first lot.' Despite the sense of impending death, most Londoners carried on as normal, looking up to see where the bomb would drop. A saying at the time was: 'If you heard them you were alive, if you didn't, you were dead.'[86]

Although fewer V-1s fell on the western suburbs, some did. Erica Ford, a young Ealing resident, wrote in her diary for 21 July 1944:

> Another noisy thumping night. About 11.45 Mrs Quine & I were reading kitchen rules, when there was a terrific crash & place shook & dust got in our eyes. We went outside to see great columns of smoke just over houses in west Ealing Broadway, about 150 yards away. Mrs Quine fainted dead away & had hysteria when she came to. She also disappeared to women's quarters & wasn't seen till lunchtime.[87]

Yet, although there were a number of V-1 bombs that fell on Ealing in the summer of 1944, and they did cause concern, they did not disrupt life, at least not according to Miss Ford. On 6 July she wrote: 'Had breakfast in bed on landing! Got up & did basins & dusted my room & went shopping. Had sunbathe in porch & did washing. Wrote to Gwen. Went up the road to deliver cherries to Mrs Clark.' Danger was acknowledged but did not cause panic. Miss Ford wrote on 5 August, when reading a newspaper, 'very good on all fronts, except the "doodle-bug" one'.[88]

There was also humour, of a dark kind. A man in Lee began giving 'buzz-bomb parties' lasting all weekend, on the principle that if you were to be killed by them, one might as well have an enjoyable last night. Elsewhere, after a woman prayed in church that the bombs would pass by overhead, the vicar remarked: 'That's a bit hard on the next people, isn't it?' and was given the reply, 'I don't care about that; they must pray harder and push it on a bit further!'[89]

Children reacted resiliently. Boys formed aircraft spotting clubs and eagerly watched them, before just as enthusiastically collecting fragments as souvenirs. One child told its mother he wanted to see a bomb fall as he had not seen one do that before, having only seen ones pass safely (for them) overhead. To older children, the bombs were one of two evils (the other being exams). As a Northwood pupil recalled, 'Revising the Franchise Acts came a poor second to a doodlebug.'[90]

Conditions in shelters, were, as before, mixed. A Sydenham woman recalled their primitive facilities: 'no toilet facilities or water for heating up to make my baby's milk feed [. . .] Adults were smoking, talking and moving in and out all night'. Yet, for some younger people, it was a happier experience. One woman recalled, as a fourteen-year-old in Wood Green:

> The shelter had three-tiered wooden bunks and Pam and I had the top ones next to each other. We brought our blankets and pillows and we really enjoyed it and we talked and laughed until we were told to go to sleep by everybody else.[91]

Steps were taken to alleviate the position of the civilian population. In July and August 1944, about a million people – mostly children, the elderly and the homeless – were evacuated. A number of deep shelters were dug, eight in all, and each catered for 8,000 people. Greater success by fighter aircraft and anti-aircraft guns resulted in many more V-1 rockets being shot down. And the launching pads in northern France and the Low Countries were being overrun as the Allies advanced towards Germany. By early September, the menace seemed to have been vanquished and many evacuees returned to London.

Yet there was worse to come. These were the V–2 rockets, the first form of ballistic missiles, against which there was no defence and no warning. Unlike the V–1s, they were timed to explode in the air and scattered death on London. The first two fell on 8 September 1944 on Chiswick and Epping Forest. Mr Bignell recalled standing outside the Manor House in Stoke Newington on that Friday evening and hearing first the bomb blast in Chiswick, on the other side of London, followed by the sound of the V–2 passing through the earth's atmosphere. Within two months, 210 had been launched, killing 456 people. The worst single attack was at a Woolworth's in New Cross on 25 November, when 160 died. In all, 1,050 were launched, though only half reached their destination. The worst week for casualties was the second week of February 1945, when 180 people were killed. The last rocket fired against England was on 27 March 1945, just six weeks before the war in Europe was over. In total, 2,511 people were killed and 6,000 injured.

The V–2 attacks were shrouded in mystery. There was no film footage of them and no sound of gunnery against them. Nor were there any air-raid warnings. Their speed made it almost impossible to see or hear them before they exploded. Press censorship was even tighter than earlier in the war. The V–2s were not acknowledged by the government for some time, and in lieu of concrete information, there was talk of gas main explosions every time they exploded (ironically, in July 2005, there was a similar rumour on the BBC news pages before it was known that terrorist bombs were being let off in London). This lack of information may have made these 'bolts from the blue' as one author has called them, all the more terrifying. Some wondered if the government knew what was happening and if they were out of touch with reality. There was no official acknowledgement of the V–2s until November 1944. This was almost certainly an error on the part of officialdom, as 'the absence of warnings and the official silence add to the apprehensions of the nervous'.[92]

Very few traces of the rockets could be seen or heard before they began their descent. On 16 September, a Muswell Hill resident saw a long vapour trail, then a projectile in flight. It burst into three smaller projectiles. Finally there was the explosion. Others talked of a trail of brown smoke and a hissing noise. A woman from Wimbledon described a phenomenon resembling 'frozen lightning, almost too bright to look at'.[93]

There were fewer V-2 rockets than V-1s, but they were more deadly. Charles Draper in Peckham noted:

It was a lot worse than what the doodlebugs did. It would take out a whole row of houses or a block of flats; the complete block would just disappear. And then, say, another 100 yards away the walls were caved in, party walls were gone, roofs blown off, the structure was in a terrible state. They were irreparable.

Another testimony to the terror was that of the young June Gaida, who witnessed the New Cross bombing in November 1944:

suddenly there was a blinding flash of light, and a roaring, rushing sound. I was thrown into the air. There was noise all round me, a deafening terrible noise that beat against my eardrums and, when I fell to the ground, I curled myself up in a ball to protect myself and I tried to scream but there wasn't any air.[94]

It is worth looking at the New Cross attack in a little detail, because it has been so well covered by eyewitness accounts. This took place on 25 November and the rocket fell on the crowded Woolworth's store on New Cross Road, almost opposite the town hall. One resident later recalled:

Out of the blue – no warnings with V-2s – a rocket fell directly onto Woolworths, packed with shoppers. They didn't stand a chance. The whole area shook. We lived halfway down Clifton Rise and windows and doors were blown in with the blast. After the sudden fright of everything around your home being shaken violently and the crashing of glass, for a few seconds there was an eerie silence. Before the dust from the explosion had time to settle you heard the shouts and people running up the hill – 'It's Woolworths, a direct hit.' Everybody in the vicinity was afraid for someone. Where are they? Did they go to Woolworths?[95]

Witnesses saw 'a great big plume of debris going straight up in the air'. It could be seen for miles around. In the immediate aftermath of the rocket, 'it was literally panic, nobody knew what they were doing'. People were running about, sirens were going off and ambulances raced to the scene. 'It was as a battlefield,' one man said. 'All this was happening at once. Clouds of dust and fire added to the scene of carnage – as well as dozens of corpses laying on the street. The smell of death was in the air. A soldier said he had never seen such scenes of devastation even on active service.' Afterwards, 'Every available hand was there to help with the digging.' The digging for survivors went on through the night.[96]

Those who were not directly involved often knew people who were, or feared that their friends and relatives were killed or injured. At first, people showed scant respect for the dead when turning over each one to try to find their loved one. One woman had not seen her young sister and thought the worst. It was an awful day as the family went around hospitals and mortuaries. They had no 'success'. Eventually only parts of the body were found and most of her relatives did not go and view these remains. Often people had to wait hours to know what had happened to their loved ones, because the police roped off the areas most badly affected and told people that they would be told when there was news. In some cases, it was three days before they were sure. Some families were luckier. One girl's mother told her that she had gone out for some fish and one of the shops was near to where the rocket fell – fortunately she had been to the other shop. One woman said: 'You accepted it more or less during the war, but it was a sad experience.' Some acted coolly. A young post office assistant recalled the dust and rubble falling around her, but she remembered to put all the cash and post office books into the safe before leaving the building, recalling: 'We had a jolly good job at the post office and it was our responsibility.'[97]

One young man who lost his parents later recalled, 'I just don't remember how we coped then.' He said that the captain of the Boys' Brigade, of which he was a member, was a great help. 'I suspect that it was having the strength of that organisation and being able to go almost every night of the week to join some function, whether it was first aid practice, drill practice or Bible class, that probably helped me to come to some terms with what happened.' For others it was just as difficult, one man recalling: 'It shook me, took me months to get over it.'[98]

This incident called on many civil defence workers in South-West London, stretching the service to capacity. As its Controller, Captain Cameron-Chisholm recalled:

> We bled the group white with services at New Cross Road [...] We could not have dealt with another incident at the same time [...] No rescue services were left in Lewisham or Woolwich [...] I am very proud of the Group's achievement.[99]

The work was difficult for those involved, requiring as it did, the recovery of mangled corpses from the rubble. One man later recalled:

Looking back, it seems to me impossible to convey to someone who did not experience it just what it was like. In some ways it all seemed unreal. There was an ever-present sense of danger. Most of the time the weather was cold, but it seemed that however cold it was we were always perspiring and always covered in brick dust. Many of us at times worked twenty hours a day and were usually pretty weary.

When dealing with enquiries from relatives, the rescue workers 'didn't have time to feel. You feel after. You're so busy, you're here, you're there [. . .] You'd try to find them but you couldn't stop because there was so much to do.' Some refreshment was on hand from the Salvation Army and the Women's Voluntary Service and many workers went to the pub once their shift was over. It was difficult to talk about their work, though: 'Nobody ever talked', one man recalled.[100]

Another terrible incident occurred at the junction of Trundley Road and Sandford Street in Bermondsey in the early morning of 7 March 1945. A baby was trapped under the rubble. An eyewitness recounted:

The supervisor told us to edge through and scrape a passage, 'And be bloody quick about it', seeing as both casualties were right under the collapsed home [. . .] He wormed his way to the baby's cot, working in a very awkward position, with an obstruction pressing on his abdomen, while also trying to direct the rescue of the father. He reached out to get the baby, which was quiet but moving, when he was suddenly overcome by nausea. He edges aside to allow another to take the baby . . .[101]

The feeling of vulnerability was apparent. At least the doodlebugs could be shot down and air-raid warnings could be given against them. The V–2s were unstoppable. With the standing down of the Home Guard in November, Londoners' sense of powerlessness was even greater. The Home Guard could not have done anything practical against the rockets, but membership did bring about a pride and a sense that something could be done. Activity, even if it had little practical value, was of great psychological benefit for those taking part.

Some people did not bother taking shelter against the bombs and went to bed instead of going to an air-raid shelter. Lewis Blake recalled:

I remember I was rather startled to find my family preparing for bed, apparently unconcerned by the threat. Somehow I expected people to be spending nights in an air-raid shelter as they were when I left four months ago.

This fatalism was based on the belief that it was rare for a rocket to hit a specific target and that shelters would not stand a direct hit. As we have seen, similar attitudes had prevailed in the First World War, too. Certainly on 19 October, three families, sheltering in their Andersons were all killed by a rocket that struck on that night.[102]

Morale was tenuous. In part, this was because the rockets mainly fell on East and South-East London, rather than on the wealthier districts, fuelling irrational class resentment. But it was also because of the effect on the capital's housing stock. More and more properties were being damaged or destroyed. Parts of London were looking desperate – akin to shanty towns. There was little money to spend on repairing these houses and little available labour even if the funds had been forthcoming. It was a dismal experience. Together with the cold of a terrible winter, by January 1945, life was more bleak than ever. Mrs Turtle recorded her concerns on 4 March:

> An air-raid warning and one or two V-2 bombs during the night, one sounded very loud indeed, made my heart go pit-a-pat despite the fact that it had gone off when one hears these devilish devices.[103]

Illness was a common result and absenteeism soared. One Mollie Matthews recalled:

> I think there came a time when it must have affected everybody the same way. We were tired, the war had been on for six years, we had suffered from it and the rockets. And this last incident, with the rocket destroying our house had its effect, because eventually I began to feel quite tired.[104]

Similarly, Mrs Uttin wrote in her diary of 9 November, 1944, recalling a recent speech by Churchill,

> I am sick of thinking how we have to sit back and take it. Mr Churchill said at the Mansion House today, 'We must exert every ounce of energy. Tired as we are after five years of war.' Tired is mild to what we really feel, and we have to do the 'nice thing' for posterity's sake and the history books that will be written about it. Personally, I don't care a damn about what the historians write.[105]

As in the Blitz, there was also great animosity towards the Germans. Charles Jarman, general secretary of the National Union of Seamen, wrote for publication the following:

> Seamen and their families and the people of London can 'take it', but are not going to do so laying down. Make the punishment fit the

crime. I hope the PM will say with blunt emphasis that Air Command will single out, day by day and night by night, German towns and bomb them as ruthlessly as we have bombed Munich, Hamburg or Berlin. I hope the PM will tell the German people that for every fly-bomb that reaches us, a hundred bombs will fall on named German towns.[106]

Likewise, Mrs Uttin recorded in her diary, on 28 April 1945, 'I hope the whole of Germany gets smashed to pieces and the Germans never rise up again [. . .] I could shoot them all like they would have done us'. On 8 March, Mrs Turtle recorded: 'The Huns seem busy with their V-2 bombs [. . .] it must be awful [85 per cent of Cologne had been devastated] but the Germans richly deserve all they got.' Earlier she wrote of the 'sound of many bombers going out – going out to Germany. Now they are getting the medicine they were so liberal in handing out to others'. Jory wrote in the aftermath of the Woolworth's bombing: 'A nice, clean war this – & yet there are fools who go on about moaning we must be kind to the poor misguided Germans.' A rare voice in sympathising with the bombed Germans, and one which expressed the thought that such raids were only building up anger in the Germans against the Allies, belonged to Henry St John. But he had been absent from London for much of the war, so perhaps could afford to take a more detached view – as could those who criticised the Dresden bombings from the comfortable hindsight of the post-1945 world.[107]

As the war was coming to an end, a new mood of cynicism was beginning to appear. What would happen afterwards? Disputes between managements and workers began to break out. The co-operation that had existed earlier in the war was beginning to break down. The end of the bombing was initially greeted with cynicism by some, Mrs Uttin writing on 26 March 1945: 'Duncan Sandys [a junior minister] said the flying bombs had ceased – he talks through his hat.' Yet the end of the bombing in March 1945 was a relief. In fact, Sandys was correct, and on 13 April, even the sceptical Mrs Uttin had to record: 'Still the peace in the air continues. A most glorious day.' Four weeks later, war in Europe ended with the unconditional surrender of Nazi Germany.[108]

Conclusion

The reactions of Londoners under fire in the world wars – especially the Second – has often been deemed heroic. The 'Blitz Spirit' has often been invoked by commentators after 1945. Sceptics have attacked this apparently simplistic view, referring to a fearful populace, the increase in crime, social friction, criticism of Churchill and the monarchy and the impact of propaganda.

Such cynicism overlooks the bigger picture in which Londoners created their own collective myth, much of which rung true. It cannot be denied that all these aspects were features of wartime London. Most Londoners did not see themselves as brave. They carried on with their lives and work despite the bombing, and so, in this sense, there was indeed great heroism. There was no mass panic or debilitating defeatism among the capital's population. In part, this was because the bombing, though severe, was not as deadly as many anticipated. Fatalities in each raid were not in the thousands (as they were in Dresden, Hiroshima or Nagasaki in 1945), though cumulatively they reached a total of about 30,000 Londoners dead. Londoners did 'take it' because they had no alternative, and their hostility was directed towards the Germans and not, by and large, (as the Nazi command hoped it would be) against their own government. The lesson was that bombing alone cannot win wars; it can only do so in conjunction with other military operations. The bombing of London helped create sympathy in the USA for Britain and a sense of hatred among Britons towards the Germans. Had London's morale broken, then the course of the two world wars might have been different. Londoners, therefore, made a great contribution to the Allied victory.

Chapter 5

Post-War Perils 1958–2007

The Irish terrorists renew their activities in London ... here we go again.[1]

After the end of the Second World War, London changed again. Many people moved out of the capital into the New Towns, whilst many people from overseas came to live in London. These included people from Poland, Italy, and, as ever, Ireland. But many more came from the Caribbean, India and Pakistan. The British government and large employers welcomed these immigrants, seeing them as additional labour for factories and expanded public services. Yet this increased diversity among Londoners also caused friction, as many among the indigenous population had not wished for such changes in their neighbourhoods. This led to hostility and London was once again in peril: this time, as in the nineteenth century, from both rioting and terrorism.

The Notting Hill Riot 1958

There have been black people in London since at least the sixteenth century. In the eighteenth century, there were several thousand, mostly servants or sailors. Yet immigration from the British colonies did not begin in earnest until after the Second World War, when, in 1948, several hundred Jamaicans disembarked from the *Empire Windrush* at Tilbury docks. This wave of immigration was fuelled by a demand for cheap labour among Britain's employers and the hope of better living conditions among the newcomers. At this time, there were no bars to entry into Britain for all peoples of the British Empire and Commonwealth.

Such an influx of newcomers – who were so obviously different because of the colour of their skin – did not go unnoticed. By 1958, although there were no official figures available, one estimate quoted a quarter of a million black or Asian people in Britain. Out of a population of approximately fifty million, this was less than 1 per cent, but because immigrants tended to be clustered in particular parts of a small number of cities, it appeared to some of their neighbours that there were more coloured immigrants than actually was the case. Government ministers did not see this as a cause for concern. They – and large employers – saw the immigrants as a useful source of manual labour, whether in factories or in public sector jobs such as the transport and health services. Ordinary Londoners, however, were not consulted regarding these new arrivals, and soon began voicing their concerns.

Notting Hill, in West London, had a mixed population. It was a rough, impoverished working-class district. A reporter for *The Times* observed: 'the area is drab at the best and at the worst as squalid as any in London'. A few years earlier, the victims of the mass murderer John Christie had been found at Rillington Place. Some of its inhabitants were self-employed, some were workers in the building industry (often Irishmen) and there were also students attracted by cheap lodgings. And then there were about 2,000–3,000 West Indians, many working for the railways or as labourers. A few were said to live off the immoral earnings of prostitutes. It was a tough district, and resorting to violence to settle differences was not uncommon.[2] Unsurprising, then, that hostility was shown to 'outsiders' – whether immigrants or the police.

Trouble began in the town of Nottingham in late August 1958 but quickly spread. There were incidents in London's Notting Hill, beginning on 31 August. These seem to have been sparked off by nine white youths aged between seventeen and twenty, who toured Shepherd's Bush and Notting Hill in cars in the early hours of the Saturday morning of 31 August. Their expressed intent was 'Nigger hunting'. They were looking for black men whom they could beat up. In all, they were known to have attacked five men, using iron bars and knives. Violence occurred over the next three days and initially the police were unable to cope with its scale or ferocity.[3]

On the evening of the same day, disturbances were widespread. These were not co-ordinated, mass attacks, but a number of separate incidents caused by relatively small numbers of youths. There was fighting between youths of different races and with the police in a number of places. A gang of 100 youths armed with knives, sticks and iron bars gathered near the railway arches of Latimer Road Underground station. They threw bricks at the police – when they eventually arrived on the scene – two of whom were injured. Elsewhere, windows of houses belonging to immigrants were broken, and in one case, burning material was thrown through a window. Luckily, this was quickly extinguished. Police were jeered by white and black youths and bottles were thrown.

Black residents did not take such attacks lying down. After two days of trouble, many gathered at the Calypso Club in order to work out a scheme of self-defence. A member of the black community, Baron Baker, later remarked:

Our homes were being attacked, our women folks were being attacked and we weren't the ones going out into the streets looking for trouble. It's only right that one should defend one's home, no matter who or where you are. We really had to fight back, which we did.[4]

Similar sentiments came from Frances Ezzrecco:

If someone comes to hit me, I'm going to hit back. If I can't hit back with my fists because they're bigger than me, I'll hit them with anything I can lay my hands on and that's exactly what happened. We weren't prepared for that kind of fighting, but when it came to it, we did it.[5]

The West Indians armed themselves with sticks, knives, iron bars, meat cleavers, and petrol bombs. They numbered about 300 in all and gathered in Blenheim Crescent and emerged on the evening of 1 September to disperse their would-be attackers in a show of strength and willingness to fight. Smaller groups of West Indians also proved themselves ready to fight back. In another incident, ten black youths fought seven white youths. A white man was stabbed in the shoulder. As Ashford McPherson, a black participant, declared: 'Well, we have got to strike back.'[6]

It was estimated that over 400 people took part in the disturbances (far fewer than in the other riots chronicled in this book). Eighteen were arrested, four of them black. They were charged with insulting behaviour, assaulting the police and possessing offensive weapons. When they were remanded in custody, the magistrate remarked: 'I feel that the peace should be kept in this neighbourhood, which in my thirteen years has never been so disgraceful.'[7]

Some white people came from other parts of London to watch the violence, and others to take an active part in it. On 28 and 31 August there were stories of buses full of 'English people coming to see the niggers run'. Apparently, according to *The Manchester Guardian*:

Among the faces, some of them distorted, some merely curious, that congregate along the pavements there lies an appalling pleasure with self. They are waiting for something to happen, and too many of them will be stirred to gratification when it does.[8]

Although some white residents sympathised with those attacked and tried to help their new neighbours, in at least one pub the chant of 'Keep Britain white' was heard, as were the songs 'Old Man River' and 'Bye, bye Blackbird'. Black customers were told to leave the premises.

Further demonstrations occurred on 2 September. A large crowd of white youths gathered on Lancaster Road and chanted 'Down with the Niggers'. One man had a banner stating: 'Deport all Niggers'. The group was swollen by sightseers but the police turned them back once they marched into Ladbrooke Road. A black man was later attacked. The police were out in force in Blenheim Crescent and elsewhere in Notting Hill. They moved on groups of people standing on street corners and escorted black people home. Some of the latter were seen nervously peering from behind curtains at the strolling crowds. They were warned to keep their doors shut and curtains drawn.[9]

The rioting was over in a few days. The issue of law and order was soon dealt with. The youths who attacked the five black men on 31 August were sentenced promptly at the Old Bailey on 15 September. Because none had any previous convictions, they received four years' imprisonment each. Their victims were all making speedy recoveries by then, and had this not been the case, the sentences would have been more severe. Other people were also put on trial, ranging from teenagers to those in their thirties. Not all were white. Mattaniah Pink, a black cook, was charged with threatening others with an offensive weapon. Teenage girls were accused of obstructing the police and using abusive language. These trials attracted much attention and knots of spectators hung about outside. Here, there were no black people to be seen, except for a lawyer – and he walked quickly away.

Local opinions were aired in the press shortly after the violence flared up, most – if not all – condemning the violence. The sentiment of one Londoner, E. Emily, is typical: 'I am sure all residents of our once peaceful Borough will be relieved at the line taken by the Magistrates over the attacks on coloured people in the Notting Hill area.' Meanwhile, some believed the attacks were part of a wider conspiracy. The branch of the Fulham and Chelsea Socialist Party blamed 'the disgusting anti-working class, anti-negro activities associated with the Mosleyite Union Movement'. Yet a representative of the Union Movement noted: 'much of the current trouble is stirred up by the more unruly elements of society, both white and black'.[10]

Much of the known responses to the troubles came from local organisations. Many groups, principally trade union and socialist parties, but also religious organisations, put it on record that they deplored the evil of 'colour prejudice'. Ministers of the seven local churches stated:

> We declare our belief in the equality of all men before God. No
> problem is solved by violence. Racial riots such as those which have
> recently taken place in our area of West London, can only increase

bitterness and lessen the opportunities of dealing properly with the basic problem.

The West London Branch of the Socialist Medical Association noted: 'it repudiates discrimination against human beings on account of their colour or beliefs. It abhors the emergence of violence against coloured people in this or any other area.'[11]

Quite why the rioting had occurred was also in dispute. Many people doubted that the real reason was racial. One Mr Dixon of Chelsea wrote:

> there is no general racial tension in West London. The worst that can be said is that there are some areas unfairly overburdened with immigrants, some of whom are cuckoos in the nest, and some of whom are bad neighbours.

Rather, more general social and economic evils, especially housing, were held to blame. It was the government and the council who were responsible (depending on one's political views), not the immigrants or the local white population. The North Kensington branch of the Labour Party noted: 'The congestion in living conditions in certain neighbourhoods in North Kensington has undoubtedly contributed to recent tension.'[12]

The remedy was much disputed. Michael MacUre of the Union Movement called for 'plain justice and commonsense' and quoted his party's policy: 'End the coloured invasion: give the Negroes a fair deal in their own lands; revive their sugar, fruit and tobacco industries, which were ruined by British Government errors.' George Rogers, MP for Kensington North also spoke about the need for some form of immigration control. Members of the newly founded Dale Youth Club agreed with the MP and put the blame on the immigrants for the rioting, annoyed that 'West Indians could come here and get houses when white people are overcrowded and have not got houses'.[13]

Others opposed such ideas. The Norland branch of the Communist Party stated that they 'affirm our opposition to any attempts to solve the problem by restricting the entry of West Indians into this country, as suggested in some quarters'. Instead, local organisations should give a lead to integrating the immigrants with the host community. Other left-wing groups agreed with this policy, usually through the means of trade union membership and activity. None advocated 'multi-culturalism; a doctrine which their successors embraced in later decades'.[14]

One voice that was limited in the press was that of the immigrants themselves. Some thought that the riots were organised, a 'coloured businessman in North Kensington' alleging 'There's an organisation behind it', and a 'coloured woman in Portobello Road' saying, 'It's the Fascists.' When a public meeting was held in which the local MP spoke of restrictions on immigration, the 2,000-strong black audience booed, hissed and heckled him. Yet one man, who described himself as coloured, but not black, and had been in London since before the war, questioned whether unrestricted immigration rights should continue: 'the British people are quite right in wanting to preserve their way of life and coloured immigrants who will not conform to it have no right to remain here or to come here at all.'[15]

The first practical step, however, was taken by Albert Bullock, organiser of the North Kensington Community Association. He gathered various representatives of the community in an attempt to resolve the problems behind the riots, while Mr Lloyd Barnet chaired a committee of West Indian residents. It was planned that these groups should work with the local council. Other suggestions were that information and advice be given to the immigrants in order that they might adapt to what was termed the 'British way of life'. Leading politicians from Jamaica and the West Indian Federation visited London to speak to their counterparts in the capital about issues surrounding the riots. Some black people did go home, but most stayed and more arrived. Those who stayed saw Britain as their home and the new arrivals looked forward to (and enjoyed) a higher standard of living than the one they had left behind.

In the following year, a political maverick, who had founded the British Union of Fascists in the 1930s, returned to the political arena. This was Sir Oswald Mosley (1896–1980) and he formed a new party, the Union Movement, to campaign against immigration. Although he stood as a candidate in the 1959 election for North Kensington, he lost decisively, by only gaining 8 per cent of the vote, thus losing his deposit. Despite some British people's dislike of immigration, those parties that openly opposed it gained little support.

Many Londoners ignored the riots. The diaries of Henry St John reveal no comment, and he lived in West London. Nor did Wimbledon resident and diarist, Florence Turtle, write about the riots. Gladys Longford, an Islington diarist, also failed to mention the disturbances. This could have been because the riots were localised. Unlike the Gordon Riots, they only directly affected a small part of West London. Second, the rioting was aimed against black people in that locality – those with no interest in the riot's targets were probably able to dismiss it from their thoughts. Mr Bignell, then resident in North London, recalled that people read about it in the press but had no other involvement or knowledge of the matter.

Despite earlier ministerial complacency, the government was forced to act. After the initial considerations of law and order had been addressed, politicians discussed the issues that lay behind the rioting with representatives from the Commonwealth, in order to preserve Britain's image abroad. In 1962 an Act was passed to limit the number of immigrants to those who were skilled workers or who had a secure job in the UK. Though criticised by the Labour opposition, this Act was popular with the majority of the white population, including the trade unions. A more interventionist approach was taken in 1965 with the creation of the Race Relations Board and subsequent legislation to outlaw discrimination.

The Notting Hill riots were not the last 'race' riots in London – there were others at Deptford, Southall, Brixton and the Broadwater Farm Estate in the late 1970s and early 1980s. These tended to be much larger and often more violent affairs, in which people were killed. Yet they also concerned the hostility of youths of all races towards the police, and some were also explicitly political – the National Front's supporters came up against extreme left-wing groups. In 1966 the Notting Hill Carnival – now an annual celebration of Caribbean culture – was instituted, so at least something positive came out of the violence of 1958.

But race riots were not the only form of trouble to erupt on London's streets in the later twentieth century. Although terrorism was not born in the twentieth century, it did become increasingly prominent in the world after 1945. Terror is a tactic employed by a movement or force frustrated by conventional politics, which cannot take to the field and fight a conventional war against its adversaries. Terrorists seek to destabilise a state by attacking the civilian population or 'soft' military targets. Capital cities are particularly tempting to terrorists: the potential for physical and collateral damage is high, as is the publicity value generated by atrocities. Another terrorist aim is to invite extreme countermeasures by the state so the latter will alienate itself from its people. A senior policeman, Sir David McNee, wrote:

> The aim of the terrorist is to have his way whatever the opposition and no matter how right or reasonable the opposition may be. No matter the terrorist is representative only of a minority group. He does this by creating a state of uncertainty and by putting fear and terror into the hearts and minds of people. In so doing he strikes at the core of civilized society.[16]

International terrorism became even more significant throughout much of the Western world in the 1970s and has remained so to date – in London's case, the major threats have come from the IRA (1973–2001) and, from 2005, Al-Qaeda. We will now look at the first phase of the IRA violence.

The IRA 1973–1976

Although Ireland was partitioned in 1921 and most of the island was no longer ruled from London, 'The Troubles' were not at an end. The Irish Republican Army (IRA) opposed the division of the island and strove for a united Ireland – something abhorrent to the majority Protestant population in the North. Although it had failed during the Irish Civil War of the early 1920s, the IRA remained a political force, launching campaigns in England in the early 1920s, 1939–1940 and in 1954–1955. Although these campaigns included fatal shootings, time bombs and arson attacks, they were shortlived. But in 1969 violence flared in Northern Ireland to such an extent that British troops were sent to keep the peace between Catholics and Protestants. Violent clashes occurred and on 30 January 1972 a demonstration (the infamous 'Bloody Sunday') occurred in Londonderry ('Derry' to Irish Republicans), resulting in thirteen unarmed people being shot dead by the British Army and seventeen wounded, thereby ending any Catholic support for deployment of troops. After 'Bloody Sunday' Catholics looked to the IRA for protection. In the same year, the violence spread to the British mainland and continued until 2001. But it was most intense in the early to mid-1970s, as it was in Northern Ireland, too.

In the years 1973–1982, there were 252 bombs and nineteen shootings in London (as ever, the principal target). A total of fifty-six people died and over 800 were injured, some permanently. Prominent politicians and other individuals were attacked, off-duty soldiers and bandsmen were targeted – as were shoppers, diners, tourists and others going about their daily business. Tourist attractions and symbols of authority and privilege were attacked. Interestingly, though 138 arrests were made, none of the suspects were killed or injured. Unlike the Muslim terrorists of later years, none were suicidal. However, it is worth noting, as McNee observed, 'There were long periods when no IRA activity took place because of preventative police action.'[17]

London was not the only British city to be targeted. The worst single bomb atrocity occurred in Birmingham in November 1974, when twenty-one people were killed. However, the casualties suffered on mainland Britain pale into insignificance when compared to those that occurred in Northern Ireland. For example, in 1972 alone, 146 soldiers and police and 321 civilians were killed there: over quadruple the number of those killed on the British mainland through this period.

In London – as elsewhere – most bombs were set off without any warning. At best, a telephone message might offer vague information, being no help whatsoever. Other bombs were simply thrown into packed places. For example, there was a spate of bombs thrown into hotels and restaurants in late 1975.

A diner recalled on one occasion a bomb being thrown into the restaurant. One man said that at first it remained on the floor. Then it exploded with a large boom, and the room was plunged into darkness. Another diner, Gerald Edgson, recalled being thrown to the floor by the blast and likewise, at first, couldn't see anything. He then tried to find the people he was dining with. Silvio Varrviso was in a Mayfair restaurant, and later said that he realised the device thrown through the window was an explosive, so he and his wife reacted quickly by getting down on the floor. The restaurant was full of diners, and others reacted similarly. Most people were calm and followed the lead of the staff, who directed them to the cellar and to safety.

Mary Grammon was in the Caterham Arms on the evening of 27 August 1975 when a bomb went off. She said that she realised the pub might be a target for bombers, but never envisaged herself as a victim. When she was crossing the dance floor there was a loud bang; indeed, she had actually been walking in the direction of the bomb. When the explosion occurred, she was thrown to the ground. Elsewhere people screamed and many had been hit – she said later it was the noise which affected her the most. On her departure she saw a man on the ground who had just lost a leg.

Martin Ellendale was the DJ on the same occasion. He later recalled that the blast came from his left-hand side, and counted himself lucky as his appliance took some of the force of the explosion. At first he thought that it might have been the result of an electrical fault with his equipment, but quickly realised this was not the case and that it was a bomb which had exploded. He and his wife swiftly left the building.

On 26 December 1973, a bomb was set off at the Victoria Palace, a London theatre. Actress Barbara Windsor was performing there, and recounted what happened. She recalled there was 'an almighty bang', and was initially shocked by the experience. Having just left the stage, she was mingling with the audience – then everything went quiet and she felt that everyone just wanted to make for the exits. So she made a joke and that seemed to calm people down; they remained in their seats. She walked toward the exit and started singing, and later concluded that she was not too worried about the bomb.

Fellow performer, Sid James, said she 'had been marvellous' and that if his young colleague could remain calm, everyone else could. Barbara referred to her childhood memories of wartime bombing as a reason why she remained unperturbed. Another reference to the war came in Michael Palin's diary of June 1974, when it was thought that an IRA bomb had gone off in Westminster Palace. He recorded that it would have been a major success for them, yet on the other hand could backfire because it would recall the heroism of the spirit of the Blitz. In 1973 Frances Partridge wrote that the bombing was 'just like the Blitz'.[18]

Many others were defiant, too. When a bomb went off in Piccadilly on 9 October 1975 near to a middle-aged newspaper seller, Ron Castle, the latter thought nothing of it. He had been through worse – in the Second World War, his boat had been torpedoed.

On 3 November 1975, a bomb in a young solicitor's car went off, flipping the vehicle over. Richard Charnley, the victim, suffered from cuts and scratches to his face and a broken leg, but told reporters that he didn't feel a thing. He was said to be the luckiest man in London.

In December 1974, there had been a number of bombs at telephone exchanges in the West End. Henry Paul was undeterred. He was, after all, a member of the British Legion and took the view that if Hitler couldn't stop them, then he was sure the IRA wouldn't either. Mr Jackson, general secretary of the post office union announced, in a similar vein, that although one of the union's members had been killed in an explosion and another injured, they would carry on working as they had always done.

Similarly, after a rash of bombs at department stores in December 1974, it was business as usual. Alan French, MD of Selfridges, told the press on the day after the store had been targeted by bombers, that whilst some people may stay away because of the bombing, the store would be open again. He was confident that business would be fairly unaffected. Another shopkeeper said that in his opinion, the bombings were 'just a damned nuisance'. Former prime minister, Edward Heath (1916–2005), whose home in Belgravia had been attacked, remarked: 'Londoners are not going to be terrorised out of doing their Christmas shopping where they want.' Selfridges staff were seen wearing tin helmets from the toy department as the store reopened after the bombing.

Similar attitudes were seen among other large department stores that were hit. Robert Midgely, MD of Harrods, along with 600 of his staff, worked through the night to clear the rubbish after the store had been bombed. He said that he and his staff would stay as long as necessary, so that they could open as normal on the following day. Nonetheless, he was very angry about what had taken place, and sad too.

The Recorder of the Old Bailey talked in March 1973 of the aftermath of the bomb attack on that building. He claimed that there was an absence of panic among the staff, who acted just as he would have wanted them to. He was very proud of them, and thought that it was in times of danger that peoples' true qualities shone through.

Heath seemed unshaken when a bomb was thrown at his house, later writing:

> A two-pound bomb was thrown from a car towards the house and caused substantial damage to my property, although thankfully, my housekeeper was in her basement room and escaped unhurt.

Next day he visited Ulster as planned:

> I was certainly not going to be intimidated by a cowardly attack from the IRA which, as with all their attacks on the British mainland, did them nothing but harm.

Heath's colleagues were also defiant and unsympathetic. Airey Neave, MP (later killed in an IRA bomb blast in 1979), wrote 'Diana and I were distressed to hear of the damage to your house and your narrow shave.' More robustly, Julian Amery wrote: 'The bastards! Almost makes me sorry we voted against the rope.' When the street was attacked in the following year, the residents were evacuated but their spirits were not affected. Heath's next-door neighbour ordered her servant: 'Now, come along, my man, we all want some tea. You must have a tea urn somewhere. Bring it along, and let me make them all tea.'[19]

Yet there were also acts of foolish bravado. Inspector John Stevens recalled an area of Oxford Street being cordoned off because there might be a bomb there. However, 'a man came up and tried to insist on going through'. The constable on duty told him not to. The fellow persisted, saying pompously, 'There's no bombs around. I'm a solicitor.' The policeman would not budge. Then the solicitor said, 'I'm going.' It was then that he was arrested and the bomb did indeed explode. In the confusion, the man 'ran off like a stag, never to be seen again'.[20]

Although there was a period after the Tower bombing of 17 July 1974 when school parties cancelled their visits, two days later, tourists began flocking back. When a bomb went off at an Ideal Homes Exhibition at Olympia, the exhibition reopened shortly afterwards, although all visitors had their bags searched. In both cases, security measures were taken and routine searches of hand luggage became commonplace and uncontroversial.

Business was affected at times, though. Bombings in Oxford Street in late August 1975 had the instant effect of paralysing evening trade in many West End restaurants. The owner of the Gay Hussar in Soho, usually a popular spot, was concerned. He said that his trade was dead because of the bombs. A fellow restaurateur observed that business was good until that week, but now business was half what it was before the bombs started again. Mr Calzada, MD of

Epicure Holdings, said that his customers were staying away and cancelling tables.

There were meetings of the London branch of the Restaurateurs' Association of Great Britain. They planned precautionary measures, such as employing security men outside restaurants, strengthening the windows and weighing down the curtains so as to minimise the effect of any blast. All were keen to reopen. Malcolm Livingstone, of The Walton, was eager that a special lunch for 150 people would go ahead because he wanted to open for business as soon as possible.

Meanwhile, some Londoners seemed able to ignore the bombing altogether. Anthony Heap, an elderly local government official, who lived in North London, was able to report at the end of the first year of attacks, that it had been 'A dull, humdrum, uneventful sort of year if ever there was one.' He wrote similar comments at each end of year review, and nothing appeared in his diary after any of the attacks in the period 1973–1976. His regular visits to the theatre and the cinema gave him no time for anything else.[21]

Yet even he showed a modicum of interest in January 1977, when he attended the fourth day of the trial of the Balcombe Road terrorists at the Old Bailey. He wrote:

> It was interesting to see all the leading characters involved in the trial
> – judge, counsel and prisoners [. . .] and maybe it will become more
> exciting by and by. But I certainly struck a dull patch today.

However, the trials did attract many visitors to the public gallery.[22] At the end of the month, Heap commented:

> After a lull of several months, the Irish terrorists renew their activities
> in London and plant a dozen small bombs in shops and offices in the
> region of Oxford Street and Soho that explode during the night.
> Here we go again![23]

Similar attitudes appear in the diary of Joan Pritchard, a middle-aged spinster, writing in the following matter-of-fact tones, on 18 December 1973: 'IRA bombs in London.' No further comment was deemed necessary. Tony Benn, a veteran Labour MP, was also unfazed. On 18 December 1973 he laconically noted: 'IRA bombs in London', and five days later, 'Three more IRA bombs in London'.[24] Michael Palin recorded on 25 November 1974 that a pillar box had exploded in Piccadilly, which was less than a mile from where he lived, and, on 4 March 1976, he and his family heard a couple of explosions whilst they were sitting down to dinner. Apparently he had heard three explosions on the same day, although noted that no one had been hurt in any of these incidents.

Bombs were exploding, but this, as with crises overseas, was merely a matter for comment, nothing more.

Bombs closer to home elicited a little more comment and on 20 December 1974, Miss Pritchard noted:

> Just after 9 heard fairly near and loud explosion – news on radio in abt 20 mins reported bombs on Oxford Street at Selfridges. None hurt. Took mog [out] at 11 but awake brooding a long time.

A year later she remarked, after hearing another bomb, that it was difficult to concentrate, though that was partially due to her need for company.[25] Palin was pessimistic, writing at the end of 1973 that the numerous bombs the IRA had let off in the past fortnight had created a sense of gloom. His reactions were more apprehensive on 29 October 1975, when he heard another bomb going off, and went on to write that there had been an attack on an Italian restaurant in the West End. This had been made without any warning, and what was worse, eighteen people had been injured. What made it all the more terrible for him was that he could hear the blast from his house, and that made the sense of danger all the more real and immediate. He began to seriously consider what he should do with his family if the indiscriminate bombings in London continued.

In 1976, the bus Miss Pritchard was travelling on towards Charing Cross halted because of a bomb being defused ahead. Miss Pritchard simply alighted and walked through the backstreets in order to keep her rendezvous with her friend as arranged. Tony Benn was also relatively unaffected, writing on 5 September 1975: 'Got to the House of Commons at 12.10 and missed the bomb at the Hilton Hotel by about 10 minutes. It killed 2 people and wounded 69.'[26]

But not all were so stoical. On 23 October 1975 a bomb went off under Professor Gordon Fairley's car in Kensington, killing him. A young woman had been driving past the scene, saw and heard the explosion, and then left her car and ran up the road, screaming hysterically. She later recalled that she didn't know what to do. So she fled the scene, though when she reached the top of a slope, she could see her own car rolling past the bombed Jaguar which had been destroyed. She was still shaking with fright hours later.

Nearby, one Miss Oandassan was in a basement flat, when she heard the explosion. She tried to escape but was unable to open her back door, despite banging and shouting for help – apparently no one could hear her. When she finally located the key and escaped via the rear, she was in tears and said she had felt nothing when she climbed over the back wall. One shopper who was affected by a bomb blast in a shop recalled that she was 'severely shocked' and 'shaking like a jelly'.

When one Mrs Simpson was going to a party in Mayfair in December 1973, she saw a package on the ground. She picked it up, but realised at once that something was wrong. She then screamed and threw the packet away. This was just in time, for the next instant it exploded. At this she became hysterical, realising that she could have been killed if not for her quick action. When the Hilton was bombed, people were running in circles screaming, according to an hotel employee. During the Selfridges' staff party, at the sound of an explosion, it was said that some of the female guests reacted in a similar way.

Barbara Castle, a leading Labour minister, was certainly concerned about safety at this period, writing in October 1975: 'Such is the precariousness of London life these days.' Next week, she wrote:

> The IRA bombers have struck again [...] I've kept *The Evening Standard* cutting to show him [Ted] in the hope that at last it will persuade him to lock the boot of our car. With our car having to stand outside in the road at both our houses, we are a sitting target.

Frances Partridge noted in her diary on 9 March 1973: 'After the first news I heard a bang in the early afternoon and thought apathetically, "a bomb, I suppose" [...] my main feelings are disbelief and detachment.' Likewise, on 6 January 1974, 'Heard a bang as I entered my front door. "A bomb," I thought and noted the time. It was, just off Sloane Street, I felt no emotion whatever.'[27]

Help was usually close at hand. When Mr Charnley's car was blown up, a passer-by assisted him out of the vehicle. Dr Ann Thomson was also nearby. She recalled first seeing smoke, then a damaged car lying across the middle of the road on its back. She ran back to her own car for her emergency first aid kit, having seen that someone was in the stricken vehicle; her initial concern was to remove them from danger in case of fire breaking out.

Little over a week later, a restaurant in Knightsbridge was bombed. One diner, a Mrs Moel, recalled that another female diner came up to her saying that she had lost her sight. Mrs Moel did her best to calm her, putting her arms around the lady and then going to find some water and a handkerchief. She reported that whilst she was helping the unfortunate victim she felt calm, and it was only afterwards that what had happened really sunk in.

In the immediate aftermath of the Caterham pub bombing in 1975, nurses from the nearby St Laurence's hospital came to assist. Peter van der Vlugh gave an injured girl mouth-to-mouth resuscitation after a Chelsea restaurant was bombed in 1975. On another occasion, Marc Colakowski, seeing a man with a leg blown off, tried to assist him by preventing the injured man from seeing the full extent of his injuries.

Inspector George Murrell helped evacuate people from The George pub after a bomb attack. He also assisted children in evacuating a nearby coach. The police commissioner was impressed and said that had it not been for Murrell, casualties would have been doubled. Murrell was modest, claiming that he was not a hero and had only done what any other officer would have done. A constable commented that he was so busy getting people out of The George pub that he didn't have any memory of the explosion.

Relatives and friends of anyone who might have been caught up in bombings were distraught. After a restaurant in Mayfair was bombed on 12 November 1975, there were emotional scenes at the casualty unit of St George's hospital. Relatives arrived to find their loved ones. None wished to speak of their experiences, though one Sidney Summers commented that all were just glad to be alive.

Mr Lovell, who was a friend of a victim of the Tower of London bombing of 1974, was in London on that day, too. He recalled that he found out about the tragedy when he saw a news-stand at Trafalgar Square tube station. He was fearful about what might have happened to his friend, so he contacted the hospital at once. That night he could not sleep, thinking over what had happened that day, and finding it hard to believe the grim truth.

Horror at the outrages and contempt for the perpetrators was a common reaction. In the aftermath of thirty-one people being injured in the incident mentioned above, many of them children, a consultant at St Bartholomew's hospital said that the hospital had been tending the sick for centuries, but that that incident must be one of its darkest episodes as children had been coming in with such terrible injuries. A colleague added that one's first reaction was one of sorrow and compassion. However, when the blood had been cleared away, another response crept in. This was to question whether those who had planted the bombs would like to see the victims of that day. If they would agree to such an invitation yet still wish to carry on bombing, then he felt that they were truly beyond the pale.

Mary Grammon, in the aftermath of a pub bombing, exclaimed that the perpetrators were terrible. She could not understand what satisfaction they could take from causing such awful injuries to others in such an horrific manner. Florence Turtle, now an elderly woman living in Wimbledon, recorded on 18 July, 1974: 'The Irish murder gangs strike again [...] the Tower of London was bombed today, 30 people taken to hospital, about 12 children, many of them seriously injured.'[28]

The widow of Frederick Milton, whose husband was killed in the bomb attack on the Old Bailey, said that she would happily strangle with her bare hands every man behind the explosion. She said that her husband would never have injured anyone else, being the decent man he was. She couldn't comprehend why they had killed him and said that the 'IRA murderers' should leave Britain alone. Her husband had, after all, never harmed any of them.

Many people called for strong measures to be taken against the terrorists. Capital punishment had been abolished in 1965, and some now believed that that was a mistake, at least where bombers were concerned. Rafael Calzada, spokesman of a restaurant committee, announced that hanging should be reintroduced. He thought that the precautions used were not adequate in themselves, that the effects of bombs could be minimised but not discounted. He felt that a strong deterrent was needed, and that the only solution would be the death penalty. After helping injured people after one blast, a doctor declared that he and his colleagues would advocate hanging terrorists.

When Ross McWhirter was shot dead outside his home in Enfield, there were increased calls for such a step, and a survey found that seven out of ten approved. One woman asked why the bombers should get away with murder, remarking that even if caught and sentenced, they were only likely to serve a few years of imprisonment. A porter at a flat close to where a bomb was set off in 1976 said the bombers ought to be shot. Although the leader of the Opposition, Mrs Thatcher, also advocated the death sentence, and even the liberal Home Secretary, Roy Jenkins, announced that he would not object to the terrorists being shot during the course of operations, such a measure was never implemented. Tony Benn disapproved of such attitudes, writing on 8 March 1973:

> The violence of the IRA appears to have come to the surface and this has created a new political atmosphere in a way. It is frightening people and fear always turns them to the Right.

However, he seems to have been in a minority.[29]

There was practical help, too. Kenny Everett, a DJ on Capital Radio, made an appeal for donations on the day after the Tower bombing. As he said, everyone was appalled by the Tower of London bombings, and hoped that this would encourage donations to their fund to help the victims. By 22 July, the sum of £1,632 had been given. People also sent flowers, toys, chocolate, books and money to the injured children in hospital. John Acland and Sandra Farmer, who were married on 20 July, asked that no presents be sent, and instead people gave gifts to the child casualties. John's father, who ran a pub in Bishopsgate, said they felt this would be a nice gesture – it seemed wrong that on such a happy day for them, children should be in hospital with terrible injuries.

The sympathy of the public was with the police, and as McNee wrote:

> In London the co-operation of the public was magnificent. They
> reported anything of suspicion, responded to police requests for
> information, and withstood the impact of death, destruction, injuries
> and shock with great fortitude.

When PC Tibbles was killed in pursuit of a suspected terrorist, there was a
tidal wave of public sympathy, resulting in a large subscription of money to the
fund set up for his widow and family.[30]

These attacks caused a backlash against the many Irish in Britain. Mary
Kenny noted in 1973 that the Irish were undoubtedly unpopular in London at
the time, and the Irish Embassy received numerous abusive telephone calls.
This was unfair. It should not be thought that the terrorists had much support
among the many Irish in London. In 1976, a number of West London Irish
Catholic priests wrote to *The Times* to display their abhorrence of the violence:

> All of us deplore and abhor what is happening. We absolutely condemn
> and completely disassociate ourselves from the kind of thinking that
> could see any positive good coming from them [. . .] As a community
> we must now stand up and speak. We must do all we can to stamp
> out this campaign of violence [. . .] We must reassure our friends in
> Britain that the Irish community here and at home utterly condemn
> these acts of hate and violence. If there is anything we can do to help,
> we are prepared to do it.[31]

The IRA attacks in London failed to achieve their political aims, though
they continued intermittently for almost thirty years, and included attempts to
murder the Cabinet at Brighton in 1984 and at Downing Street in 1991, with
the final bomb attack occurring in Ealing in 2001. If anything, they led to a
hardening of attitudes in Britain against the IRA. Anglo–Irish negotiations in
the 1980s and especially the 1990s, led to greater cooperation between governments and the initiatives of John Major and Tony Blair resulted in devolved
power-sharing in Northern Ireland, enshrined in the Good Friday Agreement
(10 April 1998). The IRA began to disarm and genuine dialogue and power-
sharing began. Hostilities appeared to be over. But just as these troubles came
to an end, another, and perhaps graver, threat arose.

Al-Qaeda July 2005

We have already noted the increasing multi-cultural nature of London,
following the end of the Second World War. People of different colours, values
and religions began to make their homes in Britain. Few politicians, except

those on the extreme Right, gave serious attention to the issue. The economic argument in favour of immigration seemed strong, and so did the liberal one. Multiculturalism and diversity seemed to bode nothing but good for all concerned. These liberal assumptions were to be given a jolt in 2005.

Thursday 7 July 2005 began as an ordinary day for millions of Londoners. The capital was getting ready to celebrate the sixtieth anniversary of the end of the Second World War. There was also euphoria because it had just been announced that London had won the competition to stage the 2012 Olympics. It was true that a shadow was cast by the fact that British forces were, controversially, on active service abroad. For, as an ally of America, Britain had been party to the US-led invasion of Iraq in 2003, designed to topple the dictatorial government of Saddam Hussein. But despite initial military success, Iraq was not at peace two years later, and some Muslims saw this as part of a global conflict between the West and Islam. Yet this conflict was probably not on the minds of most Londoners as they went about their usual business on the morning of that warm, July day. But four young British Muslim men were about to change all that. They travelled down to London, each with a rucksack full of explosives. Each man was a suicide bomber, which none of the IRA or Fenians ever had been, but which was more common in the Middle East. By the end of the day, the propagandists of Al-Qaeda boasted, with all the accuracy of Dr Goebbels over sixty years previously, that Britain was now burning in fear.

The motivation for these attacks was partly religious – as it had been for the followers of Lord Gordon in 1780 or for the anti-Catholic rioters in 1688. For a largely secular society, this was a shocking revelation. Yet, with a degree of historical understanding, this should have been less surprising, for religious affiliation has, in the past, sometimes taken precedence over any sense of shared nationhood. The Al-Qaeda bombers were also political: theirs was a bloody protest against the war in Iraq.

Three Underground trains were targeted: the first being on the Circle line between Aldgate and Liverpool Street at 8.52am, the second on the Piccadilly Line between King's Cross and Russell Square at 8.56am, and the last was on the Circle Line between Paddington and Edgware Road at 9.17am. The final suicide bomber targeted a bus at Tavistock Square at 9.47am. No warnings were given. The eventual toll of deaths rose to fifty-two and at least 700 had been injured, some permanently. Although small by the standards of the Blitz or the attack on New York in 2001, this was the worst single terrorist atrocity ever to hit London.

The bombers struck with total surprise. Robert Anderson recalled that the roof of the train was just a mass of twisted metal, akin to silver foil. Simon

Corvett reported a deafening bang out of the blue. Initials reactions were those of panic and shock. One commuter on the Edgware Road train said that many people were screaming, and the carriages were filled with smoke. On the same train was Marcin Stefanski, who remembered his fellow passengers swearing – he reported shattered glass everywhere, and people were finding it difficult to breathe. Escape seemed impossible. Meanwhile on the King's Cross train, Fiona Trueman compared the horror of the scene to a disaster movie. Her only thoughts were of getting out, but she could only close her eyes and think of the outside world. Her fear was increased by the lights being out and there being no word from the driver. Manjit Dhanjal cried out that he didn't want to die, while other people banged on carriage doors, shouting 'Please, please, get me out.'

A policeman arriving at the scene of one train noted many frightened people at the end of the carriage; hardly surprising, as the passengers were helplessly trapped. Angelo Power, a barrister, was on the King's Cross train and recalled a lot of people saying their prayers whilst breaking the windows with their bare hands. However, no one dared leave the carriage for fear of electrocution from walking on the train lines.

These people were mostly travelling to work and had been taken by surprise. Yet panic did not continue unabated. Alice O'Keefe later recalled that everyone was expecting to die, but after a few minutes some people calmed down and were telling others to do the same. Fiona Trueman experienced similar scenes. Some passengers were helping to calm others, and soon messages began to arrive that they would be unloaded from the rear of the train and taken to safety. Logita Worley recalled that they all moved to the end of the carriage and opened the rear door, then walked along the tracks into the tunnel.

Some passengers took the initiative themselves. On the train near Liverpool Street, a man smashed a window with his briefcase and people climbed out that way. Jeff Porter, the driver on the Edgware Road train, recounted the events as he led the passengers to safety. Having instructed everyone to remain where they were, he jumped onto the track himself, ran through the tunnel, and then shouted to other Underground staff to summon immediate assistance.

There is no doubt that these attacks were devastating. According to an eyewitness of the bomb-blast on the bus, the vehicle was torn open like a tin by a can opener. As with the train bombs, there was initial chaos. One Mr Bells recalled much panic and confusion, with people running for their lives.

There were many calls for the emergency services, some of which were hysterical and hard to make sense of. People were reporting that they were trapped on trains, had seen explosions or had been near the targeted bus, and there was clearly a lot of fear, upset and emotion involved.

It was fortunate that, if the bomb on the bus had to detonate, it went off at Tavistock Square, because there was a BMA conference at their head-quarters there on that day. Dozens of the doctors attending the meeting rushed out to assist the injured. Dr Holden recalled a moment of shock, but then his medical instincts took over and he found himself having to go through some very rapid decision making. He needed to do the most for the most, so had to prioritise treatment for those who may otherwise have died for want of a minor procedure.

Steve Jones, a rescue worker in the Underground, recalled that he and his colleagues were taking corpses away from the living and piling the former on top of each other. It was not dignified, but their priority had to lie in reaching the injured and getting them to safety. It was without doubt a harrowing experience. He remembered how dark and hot it was, and the smell of burning flesh. He paid tribute to his colleagues, who worked with a degree of urgency but calmly – he reported no panic, not even from the patients themselves. A nurse made the comment that this was because they were in complete shock. Overall, Mr Jones concluded that the ambulance service, fire brigade and police had worked very well together, saving people who would otherwise have died, and he was particularly proud of his colleagues.

Paul Dodge, a former fireman, assisted survivors but later professed that he was not a hero. He helped administer first aid to people and applied a gel pack to a woman whose face was damaged. Wing Commander Craig Staniforth helped his fellow passengers, as he explained in a radio interview. On seeing Professor John Tulloch, he recalled:

> the first thing I did was the basic simple checks of, 'Right, can you breathe, can you hear me?' which of course, was the other problem, because you couldn't hear me that well. I said, 'How is your body, limbs, legs, arms? Is there any bleeding anywhere?'

Tulloch's precious bag was brought to him by Staniforth and the two began talking to each other. Staniforth wondered whether he should be trying to help others, but also knew that because Tulloch had sustained a head injury, constant attention was crucial.[32] Yet some were critical of those who were meant to help. Angelo Powers couldn't see any rescue workers when he left the train, and wondered how it had been allowed to proceed when the bombings were known about. He put it down to negligence and a huge communication failure.

The above-mentioned Staniforth estimated that it took rescue services between forty-five and sixty minutes to reach them. Yet, on reaching the surface and seeing the emergency services, survivors' morale was boosted, despite perceived delays, and Tulloch later wrote: 'the emergency services were a very welcome sight now, and were wonderfully friendly and efficient'.[33]

Meanwhile, Central London came to a standstill. All buses and Tube trains were halted. Trains approaching the capital were stopped. Troops guarded key buildings in London. It was reported that by noon, London resembled a 'ghost town'. Everywhere open to the public was devoid of visitors, as people heeded official advice not to go into central London, or to leave if already there.

Some theatres cancelled plays. Parties were cancelled, or people turned up in reduced numbers, and usually only if they lived locally. Samantha Truman, at Liverpool Street Station, observed that although the place was usually bustling at lunchtime, it was deserted on this occasion and had an eerie feel. In his diary, Dr Oates noted: 'Fewer people on the streets [of West London] and rather more police, esp. at railway stations, Underground ones being closed.'[34] Even those not directly affected by the bombings were not immune to them. Gregory Edwards was on the trading floor of his bank in the City when the bombers struck and observed that it became very quiet on the floor, and he and his colleagues all had trouble in concentrating on their work.

Mr Wilson, a journalist, cycled into the centre in the late morning, and later reported having an eerie feeling. There was heavy traffic heading north out of the capital, as cars headed home and out of the range of potential bombers. He described the city centre, south of Euston Road, as a 'ghost city', finding it quieter than on Christmas morning, and found the London Library almost deserted. After lunch, he found that the streets were a little busier. On returning home he found that several friends and relations had left messages on his telephone, asking if he was safe. But this was not the case everywhere in London, as a civil servant recalled:

> It was a beautiful sunny day, you wouldn't have known anything had happened – people were milling around as usual. Even at Waterloo the atmosphere was quite calm, even though it was busier than usual. There was no sense of panic. There was the thought at the back of my mind that something else could happen at any time.[35]

Yet the normality of some places in London was not shared by all. Rachel North recounts the cheerfulness in a pub shortly after the bombings. Despite being injured she was able to joke with others and 'Everyone was getting more and more lively and rowdy. It was a great atmosphere.' That situation did not last:

> A dishevelled middle-aged man came over to our group and started shouting and bellowing. He was almost incoherent. He took an empty

pint glass and he smashed it on the floor. The jolly atmosphere of bonhomie ceased at once, people froze and became quiet. He was grimacing, spittle-flecked, crimson-faced with rage, his eyes bulging and teary. 'Bastards, bastards [...] I'm going to kill them.'[36]

An initial attempt to subdue the man only resulted in increasing his anger. However, Rachel managed to calm him down and:

He missed a beat, then his shoulders slumped and he burst into tears. 'I'm sorry, I'm so sorry' he said, and he started to clutch my hand, pumping it with a huge moist and reddened paw: 'I'm shaken up, too. Bastards, why?'[37]

It was not only the centre of London that was affected. People in the suburbs were glued to the BBC news or the Internet or to the TV news in shops, seeing each new piece of information as it was being fed to them. Dr Oates recalled that the initial reporting stated the explosions were the result of an electrical power surge (as noted, a similar official version was given out in 1944 when the V-2 rockets were falling on London). Yet this line of reasoning did not last long, such were the advances in mass communication and the lack of any need for such censorship. It was soon evident to all that terrorist bombs had been detonated. Councils were reasonably quick to post notices on their websites, giving brief news updates on bombings. Many firms and organisations allowed their staff to go home early, especially if their route was one that would be difficult because of the transport problems caused by the bombing. An office worker in Uxbridge recalled that everyone was asked if they needed taxis to get home and the firm agreed to foot the bill. This was a common experience for anyone working in or near London. As another office worker recalled:

We didn't get much work done and spent most of our time following news or discussing events. We were very practical and needed to keep an eye on the transport situation so we could get home. We were fortunate to have Internet access so we had instant information on what was happening.[38]

It is worth noting that at the beginning of the day, just after the first bomb had been set off, people did not know what was happening. Tom Parnell arrived at King's Cross station at about 9.00am in order to take a Tube train to Uxbridge. He recalled that people were being turned away from the station:

I sent a text to my friends, complaining about the trains and asking if they knew anything [...] I asked a Tube worker which lines were down and he said all of them. Until then it still seemed like there had been an accident, but I was starting to question why the whole network would be shut down for one accident [. . .] Nobody seemed to know what was happening, the atmosphere was very tense but everyone seemed to be remaining calm. Confused messages from friends told me that it was everything from a terrorist attack to an electric fault.[39]

Others noted that, after about half past nine, there were no taxis and crowds waiting for the buses were enormous; yet only rumours were circulating at this stage. A civil servant recalled:

When I arrived in London, Victoria Underground station was closed and there were masses of people waiting to be let in. It was the day after the Olympic announcement and I remember thinking that if we can't get the Tubes running on an ordinary Thursday how will the transport system cope with the Olympics? At this stage, people were angry and frustrated at being delayed. When I got into the office it was eerily quiet and people were stood around the television screens watching the news (we have television screens in recreation areas). I asked colleagues what was happening and was told about the incidents. Everyone seemed a little shocked and subdued.[40]

Rachel North recounts the following anecdote in her account of the day's events, just after she had escaped the carnage on the train at Russell Square:

A commuter shouted: 'I need to get to work!' She saw me, came up to me. 'What the hell is going on? I need to get the Tube to work!' I was black-faced, shuddering, Einstein-haired. I told her that she wouldn't get to work on the Tube today. She mouthed a curse at me.[41]

Political leaders lined up to condemn the attacks. Prime Minister Tony Blair said that Britain would not be cowed by such 'barbaric attacks', which he said were timed to coincide with the G8 summit at Gleneagles. London's Mayor, Ken Livingstone, said that 'Londoners will not be divided' by the bombers and stated that in London everyone lives side by side in peace – a necessary myth, perhaps. These comments, especially those emanating from the government, were met with scepticism and scorn by some in London. Dr Oates, on reading *The Sunday Telegraph* three days later, noted: 'annoyance (at the statements of ministers).' Yet for all this, many people in the capital were happy to display 'London United' posters in their workplaces, as a gesture of solidarity with their fellow citizens.

Simon Jenkins, writing in *The Evening Standard*, recalled London's previous responses to such calamities, stating that when the IRA bombs were exploding in London, Londoners responded without panic and carried on as normal as much as possible. Sealed litter bins, cordoned streets and random searches became part of daily life. The spirit of the Blitz was evoked, even though he admitted that few Londoners still had any memory of it – he described this as part of the 'urban psyche'. He concluded that nothing is gained by reacting in the way the terrorist wishes, by changing our behaviour.

Many of the public agreed with this assessment. Anthony Duggan had worked in London during the IRA bombings of the 1980s, and said he was undeterred now, just as he was undeterred then. A student from Nottingham said that although he felt wary of boarding trains, he had no intention of giving up travelling into London. Paul Dodge vowed that he and others would not be shaken, and their message to the terrorists was that they would not win. A history professor noted:

> On the whole I would say that those of an older generation, those who had experienced the IRA bombing campaigns in the 70s and early 80s took the events of the day much more in their stride – there was the sense that you just got on with things. The real nervousness tended to be shown by those of a younger generation, who were clearly much more unnerved by events. I suppose after 9/11 the attacks themselves didn't really take anyone by surprise; but, when it happened, those of different age groups did react in different ways.[42]

Another historian felt strongly enough about the subject to write a letter to his local newspaper and it read thus:

> The events of last Thursday are shocking indeed. What will happen next is unclear, but I think we need to remind ourselves that Londoners have survived much worse – the plague of 1665, the Great Fire of 1666, numerous riots, war and terrorism in the nineties and beyond. Although we differ in opinion on many matters, this is a time for resolution in the face of a common danger.[43]

Rachel North told a Muslim shopkeeper, 'We have had terrorism in London before, and we managed,' though she thought there might be anti-Muslim riots.[44] A female civil servant recalled:

> I didn't see anyone who was panicked. Most people were calm. However, I wasn't directly involved in any of the incidents so the

people I saw were those who had not been directly affected. There was some sense of anger, but this seemed to be more because of the disruption to people's journeys than any sense of being a target of terrorism. I didn't see anyone who was fearful or scared. I think this has much to do with having lived through the IRA bombing campaigns in London. People have grown up with the threat of terrorism and aren't scared of it. There was a feeling of 'here we go again'.[45]

There was another instance of calm, as recorded by the desk manager of the Savoy Hotel. He noted that guests told him how impressed they were by the public's unflappability and their ability to carry on with life as normal. Because the hotel staff were calm, so were the guests, who were surprised at how quickly things returned to normal.

The official Muslim voice was given by Massoud Shadjareh, who declared that Muslims utterly condemned the bombings and appealed for no further loss of innocent life through reprisals. He also advised British Muslims to avoid travelling or going out in public unless they had to, and was especially concerned that women should not go out by themselves. Christian clergy also appealed for good community relations. The spokesman for the Southall mosque gave a similar declaration:

Islam condemns the killing of innocent people and what happened on Thursday was not acceptable. Muslims coming to the mosque have been very upset by the bombings and we have been doing regular prayers within our prayers for peace since Thursday [...] You find bad people in every religion, but this crime does not mean that all Muslims are bad.[46]

Yet radical Muslim clerics had a different opinion. One Omar Bakri Mohammed blamed the British voters for the suicide bombings. According to him, by re-electing Tony Blair, they were responsible. He claimed that the British people did not make enough effort to stop the government being involved in war in Iraq and Afghanistan. His right-hand man described Blair as a 'tyrant who had blood on his hands'. Such comments did not go without criticism, with the radical being termed 'a pumped-up windbag' who should not be given a public platform.

Almost as soon as the bombings had taken place, survivors used that ubiquitous device of the 1990s and 2000s, the mobile phone, to contact their friends and relatives, to assure them of their safety. However, the volume of calls put such a strain on networks that many callers were unable to get through. Those who could not contact their loved ones began to fear the worst. Yvonne Nash had not heard from Jamie Gordon since 9.42am. On the following day, she told reporters that this was the last anyone had heard from him. There had been a silence of twenty-four hours. His friends didn't know what had become of him and could get no information, but continued looking for him. She and her friends put up makeshift posters appealing to anyone who might be able to help in their search. Another missing person was Neetu Jain. A friend began a frantic search for her, recalling that she began at University College, London, but she wasn't there. She then searched all the hospitals she was referred to, but without success, and the situation became desperate.

A happier outcome was related by a woman in the following anecdote:

> People were quite concerned and this was made worse by the mobile phone networks collapsing under the weight of all the calls. I spent most of the day trying to contact my sister to find out if her husband was okay (he was).[47]

Many people were traumatised by what they had seen. A policeman said he didn't know what Heaven was like, but was convinced he had just caught a glimpse of Hell. Another officer, who had been in the force for nearly thirty years, remarked that he had been to a number of train crashes, but was not prepared for what he saw in the Underground carriages that day. The driver of the ill-fated bus, George Psarabakis, who managed to escape with only a few cuts and bruises, was treated for shock. His wife described him as 'OK for now', but experiencing the bombing at first hand had been a terrible thing for him. Steve Jones commented that no one could get over what they had seen, but they would have to deal with it as best they could. Paul Dodge found it more shocking to see the pictures in the papers than when he had been helping the injured earlier that day. Another rescue worker, when asked if he was all right, replied that he was not – he had just witnessed scenes of carnage and corpses piling up. Tom Parnell found himself shaking, and commented that although he had always felt safe in London before, it now seemed that nowhere was secure.

With smoke subsided and the surviving casualties in hospital, discussion began about the nature of the tragedies. Some objected to the minute by minute news coverage. James Macready described it as being painful to watch and listen to the seemingly endless rolling commentary and interviews. There was also discussion about the nature of Islam and whether passages from the

Koran could be used to justify such mass murder. Mohammed Surve wrote to say that terror goes against Islam. He found it hard to comprehend that London should be the target for these attacks, in particular a Muslim area such as the Edgware Road, and was certain the bombers hadn't helped their cause at all. Another comment was that the label of 'Islamic Fundamentalist' was a misplaced honour, and that more likely their theology was suspect. Majid Hassain wrote to express his disgust that the bombings were carried out in the name of Islam, and his hope that the British would remain united throughout the crisis.

Some looked for reasons for the bombings – and scapegoats. Mohammed Surve thought that the bombings showed that the government should change its policy in Iraq and Afghanistan. Others agreed with this assessment, chiefly those opposed to the government's policies, though some were sceptical. Jonathan Notley wrote that the government had refused to change its foreign policy, in spite of two million people marching to oppose it. Now, violence was taking place in London as well as in the streets of Baghdad, because the government hadn't listened.

Yet this was not merely the view from those on the Left of politics. On the evening of the 7th, Dr Oates's diary referred to his talking with a Conservative councillor, who was:

> blaming TB (Tony Blair) for the London bombing – as much as
> I despise TB, one can hardly blame him (as I later said to DM
> [a friend] it is like blaming Churchill for the Blitz).[48]

The view in one London office was that they assumed the bombings were related to the war in Iraq, the attacks on the World Trade Center and the trains in Madrid. Not all shared such views. Chai Block wrote that he wanted the murderers punished, but didn't want them referred to as terrorists, as that implied some logic behind their actions.

Others looked to the future. Lloyd Thomas wrote that London had a dynamic all of its own, picking up pieces of its past while still being forward-looking. Barbara Mastopine, a legal secretary, felt strongly that it was an attack on everybody. Claire Jones saw another reason – feeling that some were trying to destroy the celebrations over London winning the 2012 Olympics, she was shocked.

By the following day, seven out of twelve Tube lines were working. Yet people were staying away – trains to London, normally crowded – were only two-thirds full, and in some cases only half full. For those travelling to work, especially by road, the streets were less busy and they found they arrived rather earlier than normal.

Shops reported less business as fewer people came into the centre of the capital in the week after the bombings. On 7 July, shoppers were down by 74 per cent. The weekend business had been down by 21 per cent. By Tuesday 12 July, numbers were up to about 87 per cent.

It was not long, though, before it was business as usual. James Chappell, chief executive of an on-line information service, said that the impact on the London market had been relatively mild, and no mass cancellations were being experienced. On 18 July, one newspaper had a clear message on its front page – that the capital remained defiant following the terror attacks, tourists were still flocking to the City, bars and restaurants were filling with customers and the City was celebrating a three-year high on the Stock Market.

The streets were packed at the weekend (9/10 July) for the celebrations for the end of the Second World War, too. Dr Oates wrote in his diary:

> At the railway station the train was late and so I observed that things are back to normal (on Thursday evening it was on time) [...] then went to Pall Mall for the WW2 commemorative event. We saw large numbers there.[49]

After reading about the alleged justification for the bombings as revenge for UK foreign policy, Rachel North wrote:

> It was a vile piece of self-justification [...] We were not powerful, we were not politicians or people of influence. It was quite likely that large numbers of people on the train I had been on were against the war, had voted against the Government.[50]

Yet, by Monday 11 July, with the weekend over, more and more people returned to work. Paul Williams said that he would not allow the attacks to disrupt his normal daily routine. Jane Martin was more apprehensive, being fearful of taking her usual journey on the Tube. However, she admitted that she had no choice, and felt that her fears would eventually die down. Janice Rose simply said that normal life must resume for everyone. Gerald Williams wrote that he planned to avoid taking trips by Tube, but also admitted that life had to go on. Fiona Hughes reported the appearance of normality on the Underground, but felt that beneath the veneer, everything had changed. She was afraid, and whilst disliking admitting to being a victim, she was sure that others shared her anxiety. She decided to take a taxi for part of her journey, rather than use the Underground for the whole trip. Her taxi-driver said, not maliciously, that he now expected to be very busy. A bizarre reaction came from the barber of a friend of Dr Oates, who apparently suggested that Tube trains be given 'Muslim only' carriages, which would be insulated against bomb blasts.[51]

Mr Fort was on a train on 13 July, and later wrote that on the Wednesday morning after the bombings, he was travelling south on the Northern Line of the Tube. On reaching West Finchley a man of Asian appearance boarded, carrying a rucksack and wearing military fatigues, in spite of it being a hot day. Alarm bells rang in Mr Fort's head, especially as the man seemed to be ill at ease and was mumbling to himself. Fort felt uneasy himself, and at Camden Town he moved away to the other end of the carriage.

Despite her liberal views, Rachel North behaved similarly, leaving a train when four young men with rucksacks entered her carriage, two being Asian and one black. On the Monday after the bombings, it was noted that bags of all kinds were being placed on empty seats on trains, to protect their owners from the fear of sitting next to strangers. This etiquette of modern bus travel and enduring stoicism sustained many passengers in the face of unknown potential bombers.

People showed their condemnation of the bombers and their sympathy for the casualties in various ways. A fund was set up for families who had suffered bereavement. Kimberley Lloyd, a medical secretary, said that seeing such terrible events close to home made her feel helpless, and donating money seemed the most positive way she could help. Millions of pounds had been donated in a few weeks. There was a mass vigil on Thursday 14 July at Trafalgar Square, with the theme 'One city, One world'. Each bus in London was to stop at noon, though Tube trains were to carry on unabated. All over London, people – shoppers in the West End, bankers in the City, Muslims in the East End – stopped their day-to-day activities to remember the victims of a week ago. Sir Ian Blair, Police Commissioner, drew on history in his message. He evoked the spirit – the myth, perhaps – of the Blitz as a tradition where panic was absent despite the terror, and where defiance prevailed.

Outside King's Cross station, there was a makeshift shrine, where people put flowers and wreaths to show their respect for the victims. One floral tribute read: 'This was an attack on all good people regardless of their colour, class or religion. I am a Brazilian. I am a Londoner. I am British. God bless all.' Mrs Anderson's seven-year-old daughter laid a wreath. Her mother said it was good to see so many messages from people of all religions – she thought it was a British trait to unite in times of peril. She also felt it could have been a great deal worse; that the terrorists might have used chemical or biological warfare, but feared there could be more to come.

One man recalled the past in his message, urging his fellow Londoners to remember the words of Churchill: 'Let us go forward together.' Messages of sympathy for the victims and defiance towards the terrorists were common. Similar floral tributes were laid near the Edgware Road and Aldgate Tube stations, and Russell Square. These were all later put in the newly renamed London Memorial Garden on the Victoria Embankment.

Some of the fury against the terrorists was exploited for political ends by the British National Party. They were contesting a seat on a council in East London. A newly created election leaflet put out by them showed a picture of the bomb devastation, followed by a caption suggesting that now was the time to start listening to the BNP. Yet even at this time, they failed to win the seat.

There was also concern that there might be a backlash against Muslims. Rachel North wrote: 'Oh God, save us from a stupid anti-Muslim backlash; I don't want my London at war with itself.' Some claimed that the suicide bombers were not 'real Muslims'. As Rachel North said: 'They are not Muslims. They are criminals.' More cautiously, the Muslim shopkeeper she was talking to replied: 'They are stupid fools.' But he was naturally concerned, adding, 'They have made it bad for all of us, people are afraid.'[52]

Police patrolled London mosques in order to deter any attacks. There were fears that football thugs who supported West Ham, Crystal Palace and Arsenal were plotting their revenge against Muslims via the Internet. Meanwhile, scenes of hostility were apparent. A Muslim woman, who was covered from head to toe, and who had helped survivors of the bombing had different experiences shortly afterwards. People were glaring at her. A businessman told her to go back to her own country. She was shocked by how people were reacting towards her. Travelling home on a bus, people avoided sitting near her, and a teenage girl even asked if there was a bomb in her bag.

An elderly white lady shouted at Muslim children being dropped off at school, calling them terrorists who had attacked both America and Britain. A Muslim with a rucksack was glared at on the Underground and some people moved away from him (it should be remembered that the four Muslim terrorists had hidden their bombs in rucksacks). Another young man, Mr S. Daram, wrote to say that being a rucksack-carrying Asian, he was now regarded as the 'new bogeyman of our streets'. But he declared himself a law-abiding British citizen who condemned all forms of terrorism.

We do not know the extent of the 'anti-Muslim backlash', which was feared in some quarters. Unfortunately, the Metropolitan Police figures for 'Islamophobic crime' were not recorded until January 2006 (anti-Irish attacks in previous decades were not specifically noted either).

It was unknown who was responsible for these crimes until 13 July. They were Mohammad Sidique Khan, Hasib Hussain, Shehzad Tanweer and Jamal Lindsay – young, British-born Muslims of Asian origin, three from the suburbs of Leeds and one from Aylesbury. On the morning of the attack they had driven to Luton station and took the train from there to London. That they were of British origin made it even worse for some liberal commentators, as it cast some doubt on the success of multi-culturalism. One commentator observed that there must be something in Islam that drove some Muslims to dangerous acts.

Before dismissing the reactions to the Muslims quoted above as being simply the work of racists, one should recall the responses of Londoners in earlier attacks on the city. In the period of the Great Fire, foreigners were suspected and blamed, and during the bombing of 1915–1917, German shopkeepers became the targets of hatred. When people are frightened and unable to attack the actual perpetrators of terrible deeds, their behaviour deviates from the norm. This is not to condone such behaviour, but to put it in context that we may better understand it.

Some Pakistani youths were reported as being sympathetic with the aims of the suicide bombers. A survey discovered that 5 per cent of British Muslims and 7 per cent of those under thirty-five, thought that these attacks were justified. As one said, they saw the murder of Palestinians, violence in Chechnya and Iraq, and the pain they felt was transformed into anger. Bonds of religion seemingly counted for more than bonds of shared nationality or citizenship.

Meanwhile, another method of showing hostility towards the bombers was chosen by Alfie Dennen from North London. He set up a website entitled 'We're Not Afraid.com'. This was to mock the bombers and to show defiance towards them. This was created only hours after the bombings and showed pictures of them. It was popular and recorded 20 million hits after only a week. Another way of defying terror was a 'Beat the bombers' party at Shepherd's Bush on the evening of 20 July. As Paul Marlowe observed, he couldn't imagine many other countries where there would be such a response in time of tragedy. He thought it was marvellous.

A few weeks after the bombing, Muslim websites appeared, with messages of peace. One showed a small boy with the label, 'I want to grow up, not blow up.' Another read: 'Islam is a way of life, not a way of death.' On the other hand, Muslim bookshops in London were found to contain literature supporting terrorism.

The Internet as a means of rapid mass communication was used in another way. The urban75 website was a popular Internet bulletin board where people could post their own messages and comment on those already there. Many people wrote about their experiences of surviving the bombing. This was also a way of dealing with their emotions after such a terrible and unexpected ordeal. It certainly helped Rachel North, who posted her own account:

> Almost immediately, people reading urban75 started to respond to my account. Somewhere in the city, people I did not know were reading what I wrote and reaching out to me. The extraordinary blessing of the kindness of strangers manifested itself again, people were writing back, my words reaching them at almost the speed of thought. The words on the computer screen swam in front of me; that was the tears coming again. People were sending me cyber-hugs, telling me to look after myself. I was so grateful and touched by their compassion.[53]

There were also other groups, such as King's Cross United, where people who had been in the train when the bomb went off, met up for evenings in the pub.

Two people who wrote books about their experiences on the Underground on 7 July were critical of the government's responses to the bombings. They also had mixed relations with the media. Professor Tulloch's image was used by *The Sun* newspaper to add weight to their support of the government's proposed legislation, 'Tell Tony he's right.' The enraged Professor Tulloch soon afterwards appeared in *The Guardian* to put matters right. Rachel North was acerbic with certain journalists who wanted to interview her, as well as being infuriated with Charles Clarke's attack on 'pathetic liberals' who opposed government policy. Yet she did agree with Ken Livingstone and repeated his rather meaningless slogan: 'Seven million Londoners. One London.'[54]

A rather curious entrepreneurial approach was taken by another vendor – he sold 'panic bags'. These consisted of everything needed to survive an attack. There was a canteen to hold water, iron rations, an A-Z London street map, a torch that fitted around the head and a rucksack. These found a ready market in those feeling apprehensive.

As with the Fenian and IRA attacks, although the bombings caused much death and misery, no political aims were achieved by the bombers. Yet other bombers were not deterred: there was a bomb plot for 21 July, which was foiled by the police and arrests were made, leading to convictions. Other bombs were detonated in the summer of 2007 in the West End. No one was harmed in these incidents. Less fortunate was Jean Charles de Menezes, a young Brazilian, who was shot dead by police marksmen at Stockwell Underground station on the following day. Although believed to be a terrorist, he was, in fact, wholly innocent, and though the police emerged fairly unscathed in the courts, this issue remains a controversial one. In fact, the whole issue of Al-Qaeda terrorism remains an open one. The government responded by trying to pass laws to tighten security measures, especially in relation to conspiracy and detention, though this was much criticised by the opposition and civil rights groups. Indeed, the Bill to increase detention of suspects without charge from fourteen to ninety days was quashed in the Blair government's first defeat in the Commons. Laws were passed to ban membership of terrorist groups and to end the glorification of terrorism. What will happen next remains to be seen, as this chapter is currently without a discernible end.

Conclusion

Although enemy armies and air forces no longer endangered London after 1945, Londoners – almost all of them ordinary people – have been in danger from other sources. As in previous centuries, some have been caught up in riots and have been forced to fight back in self-defence. A greater menace, however, and one which had lain dormant for almost a century, is terrorism. Responses by those under attack have varied. Panic, naturally, is one of the first responses to any sudden and unexpected explosion and to the sight of violent death and injury. Yet many people remained calm, especially if they had had previous experience of war or terrorist activity. Anger at those responsible is another emotion. In the 1970s, calls for hanging to be reintroduced were common, though this happened to a lesser extent thirty years later. Incoherent rage was one response in 2005. More positive was the way many people were eager to assist those affected by the bombing, whether by gifts of money or by physically helping injured people until the emergency services arrived. The other is the way in which people tended to be even more repelled by the terrorists.

The other question is that concerning the fellow nationals and co-religionists of the terrorists. Many feared that they might be lumped with the bombers and so be targeted by those angry with the terrorists. As a matter of self-defence, on all occasions, representatives of these communities went out of their way to express their abhorrence at these vile actions.

These bombings only directly affected small parts of the capital, though often had a wider, indirect effect. London diarists, as noted, hardly mentioned the bombings in the 1970s, for instance. It is worth noting that the bombings in Madrid in 2004 influenced the new Spanish government's policy regarding their military involvement in Iraq; but although many in London opposed their government's policy in that country, the government was unmoved.

Conclusion

Just as London's population was – and remains – diverse, whether due to wealth, religion, politics or race, responses to attacks on themselves and their city have also been varied. However, political leaders are often on hand, certainly in the democratic twentieth and twenty-first centuries, to stress how united Londoners are towards any particular crisis. Their comments are usually full of supposedly inspiring words about the bravery of Londoners and their unity; whether it is 'London can take it' of 1940 or 'Seven million Londoners. One London' of 2005.

As we have seen, bravery is only one facet of people's behaviour. A disaster can bring out the best in people. It is this aspect that is well known and there is little doubting the courage and dedication of rescue workers during the Second World War or in the aftermath of terrorist attacks in subsequent decades. The resolution of Londoners in defending the capital in the sixteenth, seventeenth and eighteenth centuries helped to alter the course of national history.

But disasters can also bring out the worst. In the turmoil of a disaster, some people take advantage of their fellows' misfortunes, indulging in pillage and theft, as at Clerkenwell in 1867 or after bombing raids of the Second World War. There is also a tendency to blame others for any disaster and to act on those feelings, however misguided they may be. The Dutch, French and Catholics were seen as the culprits responsible for the Great Fire and were attacked where they were found. Irish workmen were dismissed after the Clerkenwell explosion just over two centuries later and in 2005 some Muslims felt threatened. There was intense hatred towards the Germans in the two world wars, in large part due to the bombing. The myth of the Blitz is also dented when we note the tension that existed between Londoners and their leaders, though most Londoners worked together.

Bravery under attack is not easy. The 'heroic' story of 7 July 2005 or the Second World War shows a population undeterred by bombing. Yet people were afraid. There was panic and there was hysteria. Certainly during the Second World War, the strain that Londoners were put under – especially in the later months of the war, when there were frequent missile attacks from which there was no defence – was intolerable. This is clear from the diarists and other commentators of the time. During the plague years, many Londoners fled the capital, including doctors.

But of course, there were many instances of quiet heroism. Evelyn remained in London during the plague when he could easily have left with his family to go to his brother's estate. He was sure he had to stay to do his duty. Many less well-known men – doctors, clergy and parish officials – did likewise. It is possible, of course, to argue that many responses were motivated by self-interest. The individuals who joined the civilian armed bodies raised during the Jacobite crisis of 1745 or the Gordon Riots were perhaps only prepared to serve because they had property or other material or religious interests to defend.

Another point that emerges from these chapters is the number of times that historical arguments have been used to justify a particular position or make comparisons. An early example is Horace Walpole who wrote that he had seen London threatened by riots and a Jacobite army, but insisted that he had never experienced a worse crisis than the rioting of 1780. It was in the twentieth century that such comparisons were more common. Mrs Uttin, during the Blitz, recalled Pepys during the Fire of 1666, and noted that, though he could go to bed after seeing the flames rising, she could not – at least, not until the last German plane had gone.

Yet it was not until the terrorist attacks of the 1970s and beyond that London's history was invoked in this way. Almost always it was used to point out that London and Londoners were resilient and tough enough to withstand the terrorists' attacks. This was not just propaganda from newspaper pundits, politicians and police chiefs – much of it came from the people themselves.

But such historical comparisons are open to criticism on the grounds that they are simplistic and that the challenges of each age are different to those of previous times. The Blitz was far more devastating than the later terrorist bombings – and so was the little-known bombing of the First World War.

It would be foolish to argue that London has not been remarkably capable of recovery and survival over the past two millennia. The many crises have been overcome, though it seemed to some at the time that they might not be. This is because London is so important that it cannot be allowed to fall. London is a place to live, to work, to play, to worship – it is a sanctuary and a place of great opportunity and fascination. London is many other things, too – a place of great danger and of great loneliness, but its attractions are many. As Dr Samuel Johnson wrote: 'When a man is tired of London, he is tired of life, for there is in London everything that man can desire.'

This survey of the behaviour of Londoners past and present has demonstrated the diversity of their words and actions when faced with deadly dangers. Some acted well, others amiss. The past is not an episode to be repeated, but one to be remembered, if only for the sake of putting the present into context. If we do not remember it, others will misrepresent it. London's history is as complex as the city in which it has been played out – Londoners' responses even more so.

Notes

In order to avoid copious footnotes, there is one note for each paragraph in which there is a quotation and in the event of there being more than one, all the sources for these are brought together.

Key

Annual Register (AR)
Bodleian Library (Bod. Lib.)
Calendar of State Papers Domestic (CSPD)
Ealing Gazette (EG)
Gentleman's Magazine (GM)
Kensington News (KN)
Kensington Post (KP)
Paddington Times (PT)
The National Archives (TNA)
The Times (TT)

Chapter 1 Early Crises 1381–1642

1. Clarendon (History), p. 376.
2. Dunn, p. 66.
3. Gardiner (1880), p. 67.
4. Gardiner (1876), p. 192.
5. Gardiner (1880), p. 68.
6. Loades, pp. 73, 67.
7. Ibid., p. 74.
8. Ibid., p. 77.
9. Ibid.
10. Clarendon (History), p. 376.
11. Ibid., pp. 389–390.
12. Thomason, p. 118.
13. Ibid., 242.

14. *England's Memorable Accident.*
15. Perfect Diurnall, ff.47–48.
16. Porter, p. 142.
17. Perfect Diurnall.
18. CSPD, 1641–1643, p. 410.
19. Whitelocke, p. 62.
20. Ibid.
21. Clarendon (History), p. 396.
22. Evelyn, pp. 47–49.

Chapter 2 From Restoration to Revolution 1660–1688

 1. Evelyn, p. 447.
 2. Pepys, II, p. 7.
 3. Pepys, II, p. 11; Evelyn, p. 379; Burnet, p. 37.
 4. Pepys, II, p. 10; Burnet, p. 37.
 5. Pepys, II, p. 8.
 6. Ibid., p. 9.
 7. Ibid.
 8. Ibid.
 9. Ibid., p. 7.
10. Burrage, pp. 722–747.
11. Clarendon (Selections), p. 413.
12. Pepys, VI, pp. 110–111, 141–142.
13. Taswell, p. 9.
14. Pepys, VI, pp. 133, 134, 149.
15. Taswell, p. 9.
16. Evelyn, p. 433.
17. CSPD, 1664–1665, p. 488.
18. Evelyn, pp. 434, 438; Pepys, VI, p. 187; Davies, p. 135.
19. Pepys, VI, pp. 164–165.
20. CSPD, 1664–1665, p. 505.
21. *The Newes*, p. 60, 3 Aug. 1665.
22. Pepys, VI, p. 268.
23. Pepys, VI, p. 125.
24. Middlesex County Records, p. 382.
25. *The Newes*, issue 61, 10 Aug. 1665.
26. *The Intelligencer*, 78, 25 Sept. 1665.
27. *The Intelligencer*, 82, 9 Oct. 1665.
28. Taswell, p. 9.

29. *The Newes*, issue 61, 10 Aug. 1665.
30. Pepys, VII, p. 27.
31. Evelyn, p. 435, *The Intelligencer*, 15 Oct. 1665.
32. Burnet, p. 79.
33. Pepys, VI, pp. 90, 120, 124, 207, 192, 256.
34. Evelyn, p. 434; Pepys, VI, pp. 131, 136.
35. Pepys, VI, p. 212.
36. Middlesex County Records, pp. 378, 368.
37. Pepys, VI, pp. 177, 220.
38. Ibid., p. 224.
39. *The Newes*, 23 Nov. 1665; Pepys, VI, p. 305.
40. Pepys, VI, p. 341; VII, p. 3; Clarendon (Selections), p. 411.
41. Pepys, VII, p. 7.
42. Clarendon (Selections), p. 411.
43. Ibid., p. 412.
44. Evelyn, p. 439; *The London Gazette*, 24, 1–5 Feb. 1666.
45. Evelyn, p. 445.
46. Burnet, p. 80.
47. Pepys, VII, pp. 267, 268.
48. Rapicani, p. 83.
49. Pepys, VII, p. 270.
50. Ibid., p. 268.
51. Taswell, p. 12.
52. Rapicani, pp. 83–84.
53. Pepys, VII, p. 272.
54. Portland MSS III, p. 298.
55. Portland MSS III, p. 298; Verney, II, pp. 254–256; Taswell, pp. 13–14.
56. Pepys, VII, p. 278.
57. Middlesex County Records, pp. 386–387.
58. Clarendon (Selections), p. 417.
59. Ibid., pp. 419–420.
60. Evelyn, pp. 447, 449; Notes and Queries, p. 306.
61. Evelyn, p. 448.
62. Ibid., p. 447.
63. Rapicani, p. 85.
64. Pepys, VII, p. 269.
65. Ibid., p. 269.
66. Clarendon (Selections), p. 423.
67. Taswell, p. 11.
68. Clarendon (Selections), p. 414; Taswell, p. 11.

69. Rapicani, p. 84; Taswell, p. 11.
70. Verney, II, pp. 254–255.
71. Burnet, pp. 80–81.
72. Clarendon (Selections), pp. 423–424.
73. Notes and Queries, p. 306; Burnet, p. 81.
74. Middlesex County Records, p. 384.
75. Notes and Queries, p. 306.
76. Rapicani, p. 85.
77. Pepys, VII, pp. 296, 299.
78. Evelyn, p. 453; Pepys, VII, pp. 316–317.
79. Evelyn, pp. 452–453.
80. Taylor, p. 383.
81. Evelyn, p. 795.
82. Burnet, p. 284; English Courant, 2, 12–14 Dec. 1688.
83. BL. Add. Mss. 4194, f430r; Ellis, II, pp. 347–348.
84. Beddard, p. 41.
85. *The London Mercury*, 15 Dec. 1688.
86. Taylor, p. 383.
87. CSPD, 1687–1689, p. 379.
88. English Courant, 2, 12–14 Dec. 1688; *The London Mercury*, 15 Dec. 1688.
89. Ellis, II, p. 351.
90. CSPD, 1687–1689, p. 380.
91. Luttrell, I, p. 486.
92. Beddard, p. 44.
93. Porter, p. 180.

Chapter 3 The Eighteenth and Nineteenth Centuries 1715–1887

1. Johnson, p. 926.
2. Stevenson, pp. 5–6.
3. *The Flying Post*, 23–26 April 1715.
4. Ibid.
5. Rae, p. 141.
6. *The Flying Post*, 23–26 April 1715.
7. Ryder, p. 41.
8. *The Flying Post*, 17–19 Nov. 1715.
9. Ibid.
10. Johnstone, pp. 62–63.
11. Tayler, p. 101n.
12. *True Patriot*, 10 Dec. 1745.

13. British Library Additional Manuscripts, 35598, f38; Walpole, 19, pp. 94, 101.
14. Hardwicke, I, p. 461; BL Add. Mss. 32705, f401.
15. Walpole, 19, p. 165; Bod. Lib., Don.c. 107/2, f135v.
16. BL Add. Mss. 32705, f401; Hardwicke, I, p. 477.
17. Bod. Lib., Don.c.; Hardwicke, I, pp. 451, 460.
18. Bod. Lib., Don.c. 107/2, f184; Walpole, 19, p. 178.
19. Rogers, pp. 12–13.
20. GM 15, p. 497; BL Add. Mss. 35598, f77v; Walpole, 19, p. 106.
21. Hardwicke, I, p. 460.
22. Walpole, p. 180; HMC Du Cane, p. 85; NA, SP36/76, f.199–200.
23. *True Patriot*, 10 Dec. 1745.
24. TNA, SP44/133, p. 38.
25. TNA, SP44/133, p. 23.
26. Tayler, 1745 and after, pp. 101–102n.
27. Saville, p. 261.
28. Oates, p. 62.
29. Ibid., p. 63.
30. Elcho, pp. 338–339.
31. GM, 50, p. 265.
32. Walpole, 33, p. 190.
33. Johnson, p. 926.
34. AR, 23, p. 259.
35. GM, 50, p. 268.
36. AR, 23, p. 261; Johnson (Life), p. 926; Burney, p. 54.
37. Hague, p. 41.
38. Walpole, 33, p. 190; Johnson (Letters), p. 370.
39. George III, p. 143.
40. George III, p. 143; Walpole, 25, p. 77; Johnson (Life), p. 927.
41. Walpole, 29, p. 52; Johnson, p. 927.
42. Burney, pp. 58, 59.
43. Johnson (Life), p. 927; Johnson (Letters), p. 370.
44. GM, 103, p. 460.
45. AR, 78, p. 80.
46. AR, 78, p. 80.
47. GM, 103, p. 460; AR, 78, p. 80.
48. AR, 78, p. 81.
49. TT, 17 Dec. 1867.
50. Ibid., 13 Dec. 1867.
51. Ibid.

52. Victoria, *Letters I, 1862–1878*, p. 475.
53. TT, 13 Dec. 1867.
54. Ibid., 27 Dec. 1867.
55. Ibid., 20 Dec. 1867.
56. Ibid., 12 Feb. 1868.
57. Ibid., 22 Jan. 1868.
58. Ibid., 3, 5 Jan. 1885.
59. Ibid., 14 Nov. 1887.
60. Ibid.
61. Ibid.
62. Ibid.
63. Ibid.
64. Ibid.
65. PT, 19 Nov. 1887.
66. PT, 19 Nov. 1887; BC, 19 Nov. 1887.
67. TT, 15 Nov. 1887.
68. Richter, pp. 148–149.
69. Essery, p. 68.

Chapter 4 The World Wars 1914–1945

1. Buchan, p. 157.
2. Ibid.
3. Bennett, p. 143; Brittain, pp. 270, 288–289.
4. Asquith, pp. 34, 77, 87.
5. Coules, unnumbered MSS.
6. MacDonagh, p. 74.
7. Ibid., p. 83.
8. Waugh (*Diaries*), p. 8.
9. Ibid. (*Learning*), pp. 94–95.
10. Buchan, p. 157.
11. Asquith, p. 349.
12. Bennett, pp. 206, 205, 210–211.
13. Asquith, pp. 309, 318.
14. Tower, 18.
15. Tower, 18.
16. Castle, p. 215.
17. Inwood, p. 703.
18. Buchan, p. 158.
19. Bennett, p. 205.

20. Air-raid file.
21. Inwood, p. 704.
22. Webb, p. 376.
23. MacDonagh, pp. 266–267.
24. MacDonagh, p. 259; Coules, unnumbered MSS.
25. Asquith, pp. 411, 349.
26. Haggard, pp. 84–85.
27. Bennett, pp. 252–258.
28. MacDonagh, p. 136.
29. Tower, 2 October 1915; Castle, p. 223.
30. MacDonagh, pp. 136–138.
31. Ibid., p. 128.
32. MacDonagh, pp. 75, 130; Coules, unnumbered MSS.
33. MacDonagh, p. 200.
34. Tower, pp. 22–23.
35. Ibid., p. 20.
36. Sapper, p. 175; Colville, I, p. 20.
37. Turtle, 2 Jan. 1941.
38. Turtle, 9 Sept. 1940.
39. Mack and Humphries, p. 41.
40. Ibid., p. 59.
41. Ibid., p. 61.
42. Ziegler, p. 168.
43. Waugh, *Diaries*, p. 486; Colville, pp. 321, 342.
44. Ziegler, p. 168.
45. Turtle, 9 Sept. 1940; 28 May 1941.
46. Uttin, 22 Jan. 1941; Ziegler, p. 165.
47. Uttin, 29 Jan. 1941; Ziegler, p. 165.
48. Goodall, 12 August 1944; Ziegler, p. 166.
49. Mack and Humphries, p. 48.
50. Jones, Woolven, Durodie and Wesley, p. 4.
51. Ibid.
52. Mack and Humphries, p. 56.
53. Ibid., p. 57.
54. Waugh, *Diaries*, p. 486; Colville, p. 283.
55. St John, 2 Sept. 1940.
56. Colville, p. 292; Goodlet, X, 5 Sept. 1940.
57. Colville, pp. 292–293, 318.
58. Goodlet, 23 August 1940.
59. Turtle, 13 March 1941.

60. Colville, pp. 355, 366.
61. Goodlet, 19 November 1940; Turtle, 3 January, 19 May 1941.
62. Gilbert, p. 686.
63. Mack and Humphries, p. 52.
64. Ibid.
65. Ibid., p. 92.
66. Ibid., p. 97.
67. Uttin, 29 Dec. 1940.
68. Hall.
69. Bartlett, pp. 33–34.
70. Ibid., p. 135.
71. Bignell.
72. Goodall, Introduction.
73. Colville, II, p. 95; Longmate, p. 289.
74. Mack and Humphries, p. 135; Ziegler, p. 291.
75. Jory, 11–17 June 1944.
76. Jones, Woolven, Durodie, Wesley, p. 7.
77. Jory, July 1944.
78. Goodall, Introduction; Longmate, p. 274.
79. Longmate, p. 123.
80. Jory, 11–17 June 1944.
81. Longmate, p. 186.
82. Uttin, 30 Sept. 1944; Longmate, p. 125.
83. Bignell.
84. Ibid.
85. Ibid.
86. Ibid.
87. Ford, 21 July 1944.
88. Ibid., 6 July, 5 Aug. 1944.
89. Longmate, p. 195.
90. Ibid., p. 229.
91. Ibid., p. 262.
92. Jones, Woolven, Durodie and Wesley, p. 8.
93. Mack and Humphries, p. 144.
94. Ibid., p. 146.
95. Steele, p. 11.
96. Ibid., pp. 11, 12.
97. Ibid., p. 21.
98. Ibid., pp. 24, 25.
99. Blake, p. 98.

100. Steele, pp. 37, 38.
101. Blake, p. 69.
102. Ibid., p. 51.
103. Turtle, 4 March 1945.
104. Mack and Humphries, p. 150.
105. Uttin, 9 Nov. 1944.
106. Young, p. 98.
107. Uttin, 28 April 1945; Turtle, 8 March 1945; Jory, 19–25 Nov. 1944.
108. Uttin, 26 March, 13 April 1945.

Chapter 5 Post-War Perils 1958–2007

1. Heap, Diaries, 29 January 1977.
2. TT, 3 Sept. 1958.
3. Pilkington, p. 121.
4. Ibid.
5. TT, 4 Sept. 1958.
6. Ibid., 2 Sept. 1958.
7. Pilkington, pp. 119–20.
8. Ibid.
9. TT, 3 Sept. 1958.
10. KN, 26 Sept. 1958; KP 12 Sept. 1958.
11. KN, 12 Sept. 1958.
12. KP, 26 Sept. 1958; KN 12 Sept. 1958.
13. KN, 12 Sept. 1958.
14. Ibid.
15. KP, 26 Sept. 1958.
16. McNee, p. 139.
17. Ibid., p. 138.
18. Partridge, p. 128.
19. Heath, pp. 532, 552.
20. Stevens, pp. 100–101.
21. Heap, Summary of 1973.
22. Ibid., 27 Jan. 1977.
23. Ibid., 29 Jan. 1977.
24. Benn, p. 80.
25. Pritchard, 20 Dec. 1974.
26. Benn, p. 431.
27. Castle, pp. 661, 668; Partridge, pp. 128, 130.
28. Turtle, 18 July 1974.

29. Benn, p. 9.
30. McNee, p. 139.
31. TT, 20 April 1976.
32. Tulloch, pp. 19–20.
33. Ibid., p. 23.
34. Oates, 7 July 2005.
35. Private information.
36. North, p. 66.
37. Ibid., p. 67.
38. Private information.
39. EG, 8 July 2005.
40. Private information.
41. North, p. 45.
42. Private information.
43. EG, 15 July 2005.
44. North, p. 123.
45. Private information.
46. EG, 8 July 2005.
47. Private information.
48. Oates, 7 July 2005.
49. Ibid., 10 July 2005.
50. North, p. 83.
51. Private information.
52. North, pp. 122–23.
53. Ibid., p. 72.
54. Tulloch, p. 180.

Bibliography

Primary Sources

Manuscripts

Additional Manuscripts, 35598 (British Library).
Air-raid file, 1914–1919 (Ealing Library).
M. Coules, Diary (Imperial War Museum).
E. Ford, Diary, 1944 (Ealing Library).
Goodall, Diary, 1944 (Imperial Museum).
A.K. Goodlet – His Journal, Vol. 14, July–December 1940 (Ealing Library).
M. Hall, *Growing up in Greenford* (reminiscences, Ealing Library, 2007).
A. Heap, Diaries, 1973–1977 (London Metropolitan Archives).
J. Jory, Diary, 1944 (Imperial War Musuem).
J.D. Oates, Diary, 2005 (privately owned).
J. Pritchard, Diaries, 1973–1976 (Westminster City Archives).
H. St John, Diary, 1940–1941 (Ealing Library).
L.B. Tower, Diary (Imperial War Museum).
F. Turtle, Diaries, 1940–1941, 1945, 1974 (Wandsworth Library).
R. Uttin, Diaries, 1944–1945 (Imperial War Museum).

Journals and Newspapers

The Annual Register, 1780, 1833, 1884–1885, 1958.
The Bayswater Chronicle, 1887.
The Ealing Gazette, 2005.
The Flying Post, 1715.
The Gentleman's Magazine, 1745–1746, 1780, 1833.
The Intelligencer, 1665.
The Kensington News, 1958.
The Kensington Post, 1958.
The Kingdom's Intelligencer, 1661.
The London Gazette, 1666.
The Newes, 1665.
The Paddington Times, 1887.
The Times, 1833, 1885, 1887, 1958, 1973–1976.
Whittaker's Almanac, 2006–2007.

Published Sources

R. Bartlett, *A Little Boy's War* (2005).

E.S. de Beer, ed., *The Diary of John Evelyn* (2006).

T. Benn, *Against the Tide, Diaries, 1973–1976* (1989).

A. Bishop, ed., *Vera Brittain's War Diaries, 1913–1917* (1981).

G.E. Buckle, ed., *The Letters of Queen Victoria*, I, *1862–1869* (1926).

G. Burnet, *History of his Own Time* (1979).

The Diary of Fanny Burney, 1752–1840 (1971).

Calendars of State Papers Domestic, 1641–1643, 1660–1661, 1664–1665, 1665–1666, 1666–1667.

B. Castle, *The Castle Diaries, 1964–1976* (1990).

R.W. Chapman, ed., *The Letters of Samuel Johnson*, III (1952).

Lord Clarendon, *History of the Rebellion*, II (1849).

J. Colville, *The Fringes of Power*, I (1985).

M. Davie, ed., *The Diaries of Evelyn Waugh* (1995).

B. Dobree, ed., *The Letters of King George III* (1935).

N. Flower, ed., *The Journals of Arnold Bennett, 1911–1921* (1932).

J. Gardiner, ed., 'Three Fifteenth Century Chronicles,' *Camden Society* (1880).

J. Gardiner, ed., 'The Historical Chronicle of a Citizen of London in the fifteenth century,' *Camden Society* (1876).

L.P. Hartley, ed., *The Diaries of Lady Cynthia Asquith, 1915–1918* (1987).

E. Heath, *The Course of my Life* (1998).

D.S. Higgins, ed., *The Private Diaries of Sir Henry Rider Haggard* (1980).

G.P.E. Hiott, ed., 'Autobiography of William Taswell, 1651–1682,' *Camden Society*, 55 (1853).

P.D.A. Harvey, ed., 'A Foreign Visitor's Account of the Great Fire, 1666', *London and Middlesex Archaeological Transactions* (1959–1961).

HMC Reports, Portland Mss, III.

G. Huehns, ed., *Selections from … Clarendon* (1978).

R.C. Latham and W. Matthews, eds., *The Diary of Samuel Pepys*, Vols. II, VI, VII, XI (1970–1983).

W.S. Lewis, ed., *Correspondence of Horace Walpole to Horace Mann*, Vols XIX, XXIX, XXXIII (1954, 1955, 1965).

London Guide (1927).

N. Luttrell, *A Brief Historical Relation of State Affairs*, I (1887).

M. MacDonagh, *In London during the Great War* (1935).

N. and J. Mackenzie, eds., *The Diaries of Beatrice Webb* (2000).

R. Mark, *In the Office of Constable* (1978).

W. Matthews, ed., *The Diary of Dudley Ryder, 1715–1716* (1939).

D. McNee, *McNee's Law* (1983).

Middlesex County Records, III, 1625–1667 (1888).

R. North, *Out of the Tunnel* (2007).

M. Palin, *Diaries: The Python Years, 1969–1979* (2006).

F. Partridge, *Ups and Downs, Diaries, 1972–1975* (2001).

P. Rae, *The History of the Late Rebellion* (1746).

B. Rawson, ed., *The Chevalier de Johnstone: A Memoir of the Forty-Five* (1970).

J. Steele, ed., *Rations and Rubble* (1994).

J. Stevens, *Not for the Faint Hearted* (2005).

F. Swinnerton, ed., *Arnold Bennett: The Journals* (1984).

S.J.C. Taylor, ed., *The Entring Book of Roger Morrice*, Vol. 4 (2007).

Thommason Tracts at the British Library, 118, 123, 240, 242.

J. Tulloch, *One Day in July* (2006).

F.P. and M.M. Verney, eds., *Memoirs of the Verney Family* (1907).

E. Waugh, *A Little Learning* (1963).

P. Yorke, ed., *Hardwicke Correspondence*, I (1913).

Secondary Sources

P. Ackroyd, *London: The Biography* (2000).

M. Ashley, *Charles II* (1973).

R. Beddard, ed., *A Kingdom without a King* (1988).

W.H. Bignell's Reminiscences. Oral history as narrated to the author.

L. Blake, *Bolts from the Blue* (1990).

J. Buchan, *Mr Standfast* (1919).

C. Burrage, 'The Fifth Monarchy Insurrection,' *English Historical Review* (1910).

H.G. Castle, *Fire over England* (1982).

S. Davies, *A Century of Troubles: England, 1600–1700* (2001).

A. Dunn, *The Great Rising of 1381* (2002).

M. Gilbert, *Winston S. Churchill*, Vols. III, VI, VII (1971, 1983, 1986).

R.A. Griffiths, *The Reign of King Henry VI* (1981).

S. Inwood, *A History of London* (1998).

P.M. Loades, *Two Tudor Conspiracies* (1965).

N. Longmate, *The Doodlebugs* (1981).

J. Mack and S. Humphries, *London at War* (1985).

Notes and Queries (1876).

J. Oates, 'Responses in London and the Home Counties to the Jacobite Rebellion of 1745', *Southern History* (2006).

Oxford Dictionary of National Biography (2004).

E. Pilkington, *Beyond the Mother Country* (1988).

S. Porter, *The Great Fire of London* (1996).

S. Porter, *London's Plague Years* (2005).

S. Porter, ed., *London and the Civil War* (1996).

D. Richter, *Riotous Victorians* (1980).

D. Robinson, *The Zeppelin in Combat* (1962).

N. Rogers, 'Popular Disaffection in London during the '45', *The London Journal* (1975).

Sapper, *Bulldog Drummond at Bay* (1935).

R. Sharpe, *London and the Kingdom*, I and II (1894).

P. Slack, *The Impact of Plague in Tudor and Stuart England* (1985).

B. Weinreb and C. Hibbert, eds., *The London Encyclopaedia* (1987).

P. Ziegler, *London at War, 1939–1945* (1995).

Index